DIVINE OMNISCIENCE AND HUMAN FREEDOM:

THOMAS AQUINAS AND CHARLES HARTSHORNE

DIVINE OMNISCIENCE AND HUMAN FREEDOM:

THOMAS AQUINAS AND CHARLES HARTSHORNE

BY
JOHN C. MOSKOP

With a Foreword by
Charles Hartshorne

Divine Omniscience and Human Freedom
Copyright ©1984
Mercer University Press
All rights reserved
Printed in the United States of America

Library of Congress Cataloging in Publication Data
Moskop, John C., 1915-
    Divine omniscience and human freedom in Thomas Aquinas and
Charles Hartshorne.

    Bibliography: p. 101.
    1. God—Omniscience—History of doctrines. 2. Free will and de-
terminism—History. 3. Thomas, Aquinas, Saint, 1225?-1274—Theology. 4. Hartshorne, Charles, 1897-   —Theology. I. Title.
BT131.M67   1984   231'.4   84-1172
ISBN 0-86554-123-X

CONTENTS

For Ruth

FOREWORD

D r. Moskop was one of the last students I had before becoming emeritus at the University of Texas. He was the kind of student one is delighted to teach. In commenting upon his book I am, of course, not an impartial judge. He is kinder to the Thomistic position than I can be on the issues he discusses. However, I think he shows a fine balance and is admirably fair to the two authors he is comparing. He expresses himself clearly and ends by having made a reasonable evaluation of a current debate.

I would like to elaborate somewhat on Moskop's comparison of the medieval cultural milieu and the present one. What has changed is not merely the extent to which religious faith can be taken for granted; it is also the kind of faith that fills our needs that is different. The ancient Greeks (by whom St. Paul, the author of the gospel according to John, and the Church Fathers were strongly influenced) tended to regard many things beside God as immutable or nearly so: heavenly bodies, animal and plant species, atoms. Now we have not only biological but also cosmic evolution, and philosophies that take all this for granted. In the Middle Ages there was little faith in political democracy, which has become an American, and to some extent a worldwide, ideal. We have less tendency to worship sheer power. In addition, we have become more aware of our human power and freedom, hence are more critical of the idea of omnipotence as Aquinas defined it.

To say that God is influenced and changed by creatures need not "limit" God; rather, it overcomes a drastic limitation in the medieval scheme, according to which the absoluteness of divine power meant God's total *incapacity* to relate positively to human power and freedom. It must always be borne in mind that Thomas, following Philo's lead, held that "relations between God and the world are relations for the world but not for God." Moreover, he defines omnipotence as the power or ability to produce any conceivable world simply by so deciding. God has me perform a certain act, yet in such a way that I act freely. God makes my decision. Whose decision, then, is it? This is not the conflict between God's knowledge and human freedom but between God's freedom and power and human freedom and power.

In my view, Thomas's God is an allegedly benevolent tyrant who allows the creatures only the illusion, but not the reality, of "making" their own decisions. Without divine receptivity to creaturely decisions, there is nothing worthy of worship in deity. Let the foregoing serve as an example of my reasons for thinking that the case for my "neoclassical theism"—as against classical theism—is somewhat stronger than Moskop, in his modest and well-articulated study, allows. Granted, I am a very prejudiced witness!

There is indeed a problem about cosmic simultaneity as interpreted in relativity physics. I hold with Berdyaev, who is more explicit about this than Whitehead, that there is a kind of divine time. This must be somehow related to worldly time as we know it. How this can be done is for me an incomparably more serious problem than any discussion about limiting God. The God of medieval theology was monstrously limited and not a living, loving God at all, as I understand these terms. We could hardly do worse than that.

I take the divine "identifying characteristics" (Whitehead's phrase, not used by him in this connection) or attributes to be eternal and unchanging, even though unsurpassable capacity to change appropriately with the novelties introduced by freedom—both divine and creaturely—is one of the attributes. In a way I am, as someone has said, an "anti-Thomistic Thomist," for I admire and with qualifications accept the Thomistic doctrine that there is a divine absoluteness, independence, and immutability. However, a change in contingent qualities is one thing, and a change in necessary attributes, including the one that specifies *how* God can change, is quite another. God is necessarily God, and no empirical, contingent truth could conflict with God's existence or change the divine attributes. Hence relativity physics could not settle the truth of theism as such, whether defined as in classical, or as in neoclassical theism. Nevertheless, no fact apparently contradictory to a proposed theism and appearing as an empirical truth in current physics can leave the theist altogether comfortable.

At present there is a complication, in that quantum theory is not yet definitively united with relativity theory. One sign of this is Bell's Theorem, which seems to contradict the relativity axiom: there is no influence faster than the speed of light. Until this paradox is clarified, it may be premature to try to deal with the theological problem involved.

Moskop and I agree on one point: in metaphysics it is never a question of a verbal contradiction by itself settling the fate of a doctrine. One must be sure that the intuition the thinker is trying to express has no other way of expressing itself so as to avoid the inconsistency. Definitive refutation, if it is possible at all, must apply two or three criteria, not just one. The question is not, can inconsistency be avoided, but rather can it be avoided without rendering the doctrine so vague, or so unrelated to other convictions the theorist is seeking to defend, as to deprive it of its intended value? Moskop shows that a Thomist must drastically attenuate the positive content of his assertions to avoid fairly obvious inconsistencies. I believe that there is a better way for a theist to proceed, unless indeed there is no truth in theism. Yet, to repeat, what is called absoluteness, independence, or immutability does correctly describe, not God, but an abstract aspect of God. Much that Aquinas says is true of this aspect.

I cordially recommend this illuminating and stimulating work.   *Charles Hartshorne*

INTRODUCTION

This book will investigate a perennial problem for theories of the divine nature, that of reconciling divine
omniscience and human freedom. I will argue that the problem is
a serious one, but that two accounts of the divine nature are able
to resolve it. These two accounts, the classical doctrine of St.
Thomas Aquinas and the contemporary theory of Charles Hartshorne, will then be evaluated in turn.

Though theoretical inquiry into the nature and attributes of
God has long played a prominent role in Western theology, at least
one major theological tradition would find such an inquiry use-
less. This tradition, called the "logic of obedience" by Frederick
Ferré and exemplified in the writings of Karl Barth and T. F. Tor-
rance, holds that human beings are fundamentally unable to
grasp the concept of God and must simply acknowledge in the
Word of God a "higher" rationality beyond their comprehension.[1]
According to this view, human theological language is the una-
voidably mysterious and even nonsensical vehicle through which
God calls his people to faith and obedience.

---

[1]Frederick Ferré, *Language, Logic and God* (New York: Harper and Row,
1961) 78-93.

This tradition posits a wide chasm between human reason and divine truth, a chasm only God can bridge through the gift of faith in his mysterious Word. Hence any attempt based on human reason to investigate the concept of God would be both fruitless and presumptuous. There are, however, serious shortcomings in this view of religious belief. If no human language can describe God at all accurately or meaningfully, then any language applied to God would seem to be as good as any other, or *none at all*. How can human beings have a true belief if it cannot be expressed, if any words used to express it coherently are completely unable to do so? The theologian may respond that it is the divine origin of the Word of God that guarantees its truth; yet no infallible and independent method exists for establishing the divine origin of a purported revelation. By thus shielding its revelation from all critical scrutiny, the logic of obedience cannot object to a similar exemption from scrutiny for any claimed revelation, no matter how outlandish from the perspective of mere human reason.

In contrast to the logic of obedience, this book will attempt to demonstrate the value of reason in analyzing and understanding the concept of God. It will undertake a close investigation of a particular problem—the potential inconsistency of divine omniscience and human freedom—and of its solution according to two very different views of the divine nature proposed by Aquinas and Hartshorne. A direct comparison of these two doctrines both in their approach to this particular problem and in their broader strengths and weaknesses will, it is hoped, serve the end of thinking and speaking more clearly about the object of religious faith and worship.

Why have I chosen to focus on precisely these two theories of God out of a heritage so rich in systematic theology? The reasons are based on the nature of the problem analyzed, the stature of the two theories, and my personal interests. First of all, as I will argue in succeeding chapters, the theories of Aquinas and Hartshorne are able to offer convincing solutions to the problem of reconciling divine omniscience and human freedom. There are, of course, other solutions, but as I will argue on succeeding pages, one of the most popular of these, the compatibilist alternative, creates even more serious problems in other areas.

Second, these two theories are carefully articulated positions, widely discussed and professed by contemporary theologians. Aquinas's theory is likely the most well known and influential of the medieval scholastic doctrines of God; it has become the semiofficial position of the Roman Catholic Church.[2] Despite foreshadowings in the writings of a few scholars,[3] Hartshorne's conception of God, based on his interpretation of the metaphysics of Alfred North Whitehead, is largely novel. Nevertheless, it has attracted considerable attention in recent decades among Protestant and even some Catholic theologians and philosophers.[4] Recent years have witnessed a growing debate between proponents of the two positions, including attempts to find some common ground between them. I will use some of these recent contributions in an attempt to clarify and evaluate the two doctrines.

Third, but probably not least important for my choice of these two theories, are personal reasons. My Catholic background and training inspired in me a strong interest in theological issues. Familiar with many features of the Thomistic conception of God in an informal way, I was anxious to pursue a more formal study of Aquinas. My introduction to the thought of Charles Hartshorne

-----

[2]Thomas is the only person mentioned in the Code of Canon Law, which enjoins that priests of the Catholic Church should receive their theological and philosophical instruction "according to the method, doctrine and principles of the Angelic Doctor." See "Thomas Aquinas, St.," *New Catholic Encyclopedia* (New York: McGraw-Hill, 1967) 14:109.

[3]See *Philosophers Speak of God*, ed. Charles Hartshorne and William Reese (Chicago: University of Chicago Press, 1953), especially chs. 6 and 7, for a survey of these writers.

[4]See, for example, John B. Cobb, *A Christian Natural Theology* (Philadelphia: Westminster Press, 1965); Schubert M. Ogden, *The Reality of God* (New York: Harper and Row, 1966); W. Norman Pittenger, *God In Process* (London: SCM Press, 1967); W. Norris Clarke, S. J., "A New Look at the Immutability of God," in *God Knowable and Unknowable*, ed. Robert J. Roth (New York: Fordham University Press, 1973); Joseph Donceel, S. J., "Second Thoughts on the Nature of God," *Thought* 46 (1971): 346-70; Anthony J. Kelly, "God: How Near a Relation?" *Thomist* 34 (1970): 191-229; Walter E. Stokes, S. J., "Whitehead's Challenge to Theistic Realism," *New Scholasticism* 38 (1964): 1-21; and Barry L. Whitney, "Divine Immutability in Process Philosophy and Contemporary Thomism," *Horizons* 7 (1980): 49-68.

was as a student of his at the University of Texas at Austin. I was most impressed with the breadth and depth of Dr. Hartshorne's knowledge and with his spirited defense of his views. The present study, then, concentrates on two thinkers who have played central roles in my own intellectual and philosophical development.

To give readers some idea of the overall structure of the book before moving to the arguments themselves, I will provide a brief chapter-by-chapter summary. The book is divided into five chapters. Chapter one offers two arguments for the incompatibility of divine omniscience and human freedom, one by Aquinas and one by Nelson Pike. These arguments, I will maintain, do establish an incompatibility between any doctrine of divine omniscience that includes divine foreknowledge and a libertarian doctrine of human freedom. Several approaches to this problem are examined, and it is argued that the strategies adopted by Aquinas and Hartshorne offer the most promising solutions. Chapters two and three are devoted to Thomas's doctrine of God: chapter two considers his account of eternal knowledge and chapter three his account of eternal will and action. Each of these chapters contains a review and critical evaluation of the doctrine. In similar fashion, chapter four contains an outline of Hartshorne's doctrine of God and a survey of criticisms of that doctrine. Finally chapter five reviews the major arguments considered in the book and uses the general criteria of internal consistency, conceivability, and harmony with other areas of knowledge and experience to argue for the overall preferability of Hartshorne's account.

ACKNOWLEDGMENTS

I have incurred many debts in writing this book. First, I wish to express my heartfelt gratitude to Charles Hartshorne for inspiring much of my inquiry, for spiritedly discussing and defending his views with me, and for writing an excellent foreword to the volume.

An earlier version of the work was my doctoral dissertation at the University of Texas at Austin. I owe special thanks to Robert Kane, my dissertation advisor, for carefully guiding and encouraging my work from first conception to final product. The other members of my committee, Brian Cooney, Louis Mackey, and Ernest Kaulbach, read several drafts of the manuscript and made many constructive comments and criticisms for which I am most grateful.

My sincere thanks go also to my colleagues and friends Tristram Engelhardt, Loretta Kopelman and Todd Savitt for their steadfast support and valuable advice.

I am much obliged to Joanne Stoddard for fast and accurate typing of the entire manuscript and for cheerfully incorporating the inevitable revisions. Thanks are also due to Susan Carini of Mercer University Press for her encouragement and expert editorial assistance.

Finally, my deepest thanks go to my parents, Charles and Cornelia Moskop, for their constant support of my scholarly pursuits, and to my wife Ruth, without whose love, encouragement and assistance the book would not have been completed.

John Moskop

CHAPTER ONE

OMNISCIENCE AND HUMAN FREEDOM

The problem of reconciling divine omniscience and human freedom is surely a venerable one; it is discussed by almost every major Western metaphysician since Augustine. Roughly stated, the problem consists in showing that although God has eternal knowledge of every action that each person will perform, persons are nevertheless able to choose freely what actions they will perform and are therefore responsible for their actions. In this chapter, I will discuss two statements of this problem, one classical, from the *Summa Theologiae* of Thomas Aquinas, and one contemporary, made by Nelson Pike in his book *God and Timelessness*. I will attempt to show that at least one obvious interpretation of the doctrines of omniscience and freedom does render these doctrines incompatible. Finally, I will indicate what I take to be the two most promising ways to avoid the conclusion that divine omniscience and human freedom are incompatible.

THE PROBLEM AND ITS
SOLUTION IN AQUINAS

In a key section of his account of divine knowledge, Aquinas considers the following objection to his claim that God knows contingent future events:

> Further, in a conditional proposition, if the antecedent is absolutely necessary the consequent is absolutely necessary; for the antecedent stands to the consequent as premises to conclusion. But from necessary premises, only a necessary conclusion can follow, as is proved in the *Posterior Analytics*. Now the following is a conditional that is true: If God knew that this is going to happen it will happen—because knowledge is only of what is true. And its antecedent is absolutely necessary: first, because it is eternal, and also because it is expressed as having taken place. Therefore, the consequent is absolutely necessary. Therefore whatever is known by God is necessary; and thus God has no knowledge of contingent events.[1]

The argument of this passage (henceforward called Argument A) proceeds as follows:

> (1) In a conditional proposition, if the antecedent is absolutely necessary, the consequent is absolutely necessary. (2) If God knew that x will happen, x will happen. (3) "God knew that x will happen" is absolutely necessary. Therefore, (4) "x will happen" is absolutely necessary.[2]

---

[1] "Præterea, omnis conditionalis cujus antecedens est necessarium absolute, consequens est necessarium absolute; sic enim se habet antecedens ad consequens sicut principia ad conclusionem. Ex principiis autem necessariis non sequitur conclusio nisi necessaria, ut in *Poster.* [75a4] probatur. Sed hæc est quædam conditionalis vera: *Si Deus scivit hoc futurum esse, hoc erit*: quia scientia non est nisi verorum. Hujus autem conditionalis antecedens est necessarium absolute: tum quia est æternum; tum quia significatur ut præteritum. Ergo et consequens est necessarium absolute. Ergo quidquid scitur a Deo est necessarium; et sic scientia Dei non est contingentium." *Summa Theologiae* 1a. 14, 13, 2, Blackfriars ed. (New York: McGraw-Hill, 1964-1976) 4:46-47. Hereafter, references to the *Summa Theologiae* will contain part, question, article, and, where appropriate, objection or reply, e.g., 1a2ae. 5, 1; 1a. 14, 13, ad 1. All quotations from the *Summa Theologiae* will be taken from the Blackfriars edition. Reference to this edition, abbreviated "B," will be given in parentheses after the quotation. Essentially the same objection and reply may be found at *1 Sent.* 38, 1, 5, 4 (Parma edition) 6:316-18 and *de Verit.* 2, 12, 7 (Chicago: Regnery, 1952) 1:116-23.

[2] The formal structure of this argument, where a is "God knew that x will happen" and b is "x will happen," is: (1) $(N(p \supset q) \cdot Np) \supset Nq$; (2) $N(a \supset b)$; (3) Na; (4) Nb.

Premise (1) of this argument is supported by an appeal to Aristotle's claim that only a necessary conclusion can follow from necessary premises. This premise is a thesis of all standard modal systems.[3] Premise (2) is based on the claim that "knowledge is only of what is true," or in other words, "A knows p" entails "p is true."

Premise (3) is said to derive from the fact that God's knowledge of events is eternal and is expressed as already achieved, that is, as past. Such knowledge of events before their occurrence is called 'foreknowledge'. According to Argument A, therefore, divine foreknowledge of any future event x logically implies that x will happen.

A few words should be said at the outset about Thomas's use of the term 'necessary' (*necessarium*) in this argument. Thomas attributes necessity both to propositions and to things. The former type of attribution has been given the name 'necessity *de dicto*', the latter, 'necessity *de re*'.[4] In the above passage and his reply to it, Thomas uses both kinds of attribution, and it is sometimes difficult to determine which kind he intends in a particular instance. In my restatement of the argument, I have used necessity *de dicto*. How one interprets the necessity involved is not crucial to the outcome of the argument in this case, however, since it seems clear that Thomas accepts the inference from the *de dicto* necessity of "x will happen" to the claim that x is necessary *de re*.[5]

Thomas seems to overstate the case somewhat in claiming that either half of the conditional "If God knew that x will happen, x will happen" is *absolutely* necessary, since he would surely ad-

---

[3] It is derivable even in the weak system T from the axiom "$N(p \supset q) \supset (Np \supset Nq)$" and the law of importation. See G. E. Hughes and M. J. Cresswell, *An Introduction to Modal Logic* (London: Methuen, 1968) 30-31.

[4] For an extended statement and defense of the distinction between necessity *de dicto* and necessity *de re*, see Alvin Plantinga, *The Nature of Necessity* (Oxford: Clarendon Press, 1974).

[5] Thomas uses the *de dicto-de re* distinction to answer a later objection in this same article (1a. 14, 13, 3). There he argues that the *de dicto* necessity of the conditional proposition "All things known by God must necessarily be" does not, in itself, entail the *de re* necessity of any event.

mit that under certain conditions—as, for example, if God did not will or permit an event—that event would not have been a part of his knowledge. The necessity in question, therefore, cannot be logical necessity, since the proposition "God knew that x will happen" would be logically necessary only if it could not fail to be true no matter what conditions obtain. In this case, the necessity seems to be more like causal or natural necessity than logical necessity. It should not, however, be confused with causal necessity, since the proposition does not depend on the view—also held by Thomas—that divine knowledge, together with will, is the *cause* of events. Rather, the necessity seems to derive from the fact that God's knowledge is eternal and is located in the past relative to the event. Arthur Prior describes this time-dependent sense of 'necessary' as "now-unpreventable."[6]

Argument A, generalized to include all worldly events, is meant to show that divine foreknowledge is incompatible with contingent events. Among contingent events, Thomas includes human free actions.[7] Thus Argument A concludes that any free action cannot be known in advance by God, and conversely, any action known in advance by God cannot be free. Since Thomas holds both that God knows everything (including all human actions) and that some human actions are free, he seeks to show that Argument A is unsound.

Thomas seems to have taken Argument A quite seriously, for he offers a very careful reply to it. In his reply Thomas first defends Argument A against the following three objections. First, some[8] claim against premise (3) that the proposition "God knew that x will happen" is not necessary but contingent, since it refers in part to the future. In reply, Thomas points out that "what had

---

[6]Arthur Prior, "The Formalities of Omniscience," *Philosophy* 37 (1962): 119.

[7]This is clearly stated in the *Sed contra* of the article: "Sed contra est quod dicitur: *Qui finxit singillatim corda eorum, qui intelligit omnia opera eorum,* scilicet hominum. Sed opera hominum sunt contingentia, utpote libero arbitrio subjecta. Ergo Deus scit futura contingentia." (B 4:46).

[8]Cf. Bonaventure, *1 Sent.* 38, 2, 2 (Quaracchi, 1882) 1:677-79.

a reference to a future event must have had it."[9] By this phrase Thomas seems to be referring to the fact that even though its object is a future event, God's knowledge is itself necessary in the sense that it is past, hence now unpreventable.[10]

Second, others reject the same premise (3) on the grounds that "God knew that x will happen" is contingent because it has a contingent part, namely, "x will happen." But, Thomas replies, the "principal part" of this proposition is "God knew." This part is necessary, and the necessity of the whole proposition derives from it, irrespective of what constitutes the object of God's knowledge. Thus in his replies to both of these objections, Thomas defends the necessity of premise (3). He bases its necessity on the fact that God's knowledge is eternal and is located in the past.

Third, still others[11] challenge premise (2) of Argument A, holding that even if the antecedent ("God knew that x will happen") is absolutely necessary, it does not follow that the consequent ("x will happen") is necessary, since the antecedent is only the remote cause of the consequent. Thomas, however, denies that the comparison between divine causality and remote causes in nature applies in this case. He points out that if it did apply, premise (2) would not only be not necessary, but false as well, since contingent effects do not always follow from remote necessary causes, as is manifest in his example of the false conditional, "If the sun is moving, the grass will grow."[12] Thomas has, in effect, two reasons for denying this third objection: first, its appeal to a causal

---

[9]"Id quod habuit respectum ad futurum, necesse est habuisse," 1a. 14, 13 ad 2 (B 4:48).

[10]Thomas adds the following words to the above phrase: "licet etiam futurum non sequatur quandoque." This last comment seems misleading, however, since the gist of the argument is that given a past state of *knowledge* regarding a future event, that event *will* always follow. Thomas's reply to Albert and Bonaventure in the parallel passage at *1 Sent.* 38, 1, 5 ad 4 is clearer on this point: "verum enim est determinate Deum aliquid futurum nunc scire; et ita sequitur quod consequens non possit poni non esse, etiam absolute sumptum; et multo minus quod possit contingere non esse" (Parma 6:318).

[11]Alexander of Hales, *Summa Theol.* 1, 171 ad 4 (Quaracchi, 1924) 1:254.

[12]"Si sol movetur, herba germinabit," 1a. 14, 13 ad 2 (B 4:48).

relationship between God and his effects cannot establish the contingency of those effects, since the divine causality, unlike remote necessary causes in nature, is universally efficacious;[13] and second, there is no reason to appeal to causality here at all, since the epistemic relation between God and creatures is by itself sufficient to ground premise (2).

Thus far in his reply to Argument A, Thomas has *defended* the key premises (2) and (3). He now goes on to *attack* the argument by distinguishing two modes of existence of a contingent future event, namely: (1) its existence in itself, as already actual, and (2) its existence in the mind or soul of one who knows it. Since Argument A focuses on God's knowledge, Thomas holds that the mode of existence of the event in the argument should be understood to be of the latter sort, that is, existence in the mind of God. In its condition as an object of the divine knowledge, however, each event is present, since all things are eternally present to the divine gaze.[14] As such, all events are necessary, but their necessity is the necessity of the *present*, not of the past. Thomas applies to these events Aristotle's statement, "That which is, when it is, must necessarily be."[15] This is, however, a very weak sense of necessity; it is compatible with the prior contingency of each event, and in the case of human actions, with freedom. In other words, the fact that an event now occurring cannot *not* be occurring is compatible with the claim that prior to its occurrence the event may or may not have occurred as well as with the claim that the event was the product of free will. The objection formulated in Argument A, therefore, cannot defeat Thomas's contention in this article that God knows contingent future events.

In effect, then, Thomas answers Argument A by maintaining that experience in time is foreign to the divine consciousness, and

---

[13] 1a. 19, 6.

[14] The notion of divine "presentiality" employed here is introduced at 1a. 8, 3 (B 2:120): "[Deus] est per praesentiam in omnibus inquantum omnia nuda sunt et aperta oculis ejus." Thomas explains that God also exists in a special way—by grace—in those rational creatures who know and love him.

[15] "Omne quod est, quando est, necesse est esse" 1a. 14, 13 ad 2 (B 4:50). Cf. Aristotle, *De Interpretatione* 1, 9, 19a23.

hence the use of past and future tenses to describe God's knowledge and the relation of events to God is, strictly speaking, incor-
rect. In the body of this article, Thomas contends that divine
knowledge is eternally and simultaneously whole.[16] Consequently, all events are eternally present to God. Thomas rejects
premise (3), then, because it attributes a *past* mental state to God
and *future* existence to the event he knows, i.e., "God *knew* that *x*
will happen." Thomas is committed to replacing premise (3) with
present-tense expressions like, "If God knows something, it is."[17]
He concludes that God's knowledge makes events necessary only
in the weak sense in which all present events are necessary. Since
God's knowledge is not to be viewed as a prior determining condition, events can remain contingent in the sense that they are not
determined by their proximate causes.[18]

In view of Thomas's careful reply to Argument A, it is worth
noting exactly where he accepts that argument and where he
finds fault with it. As we have seen in his response to several objections made by others, Thomas agrees with Argument A that divine knowledge is necessary and that divine *fore*knowledge (i.e.,
knowledge of future events) *would* render those events necessary.
In other words, Thomas argues that an event cannot be contingent—and hence a human action cannot be free—if it is entailed
by an antecedent event, in this case, an antecedent state of divine
knowledge.[19] Thomas denies, however, that God has knowledge of

---

[16]"Sua cognitio mensuratur aeternitate, sicut etiam suum esse; aeternitas
autem tota simul existens ambit totum tempus" 1a. 14, 13c (B 4:46).

[17]Thomas does, in fact, make such a suggestion in a parallel passage in *de
Veritate*: "Quamvis autem res in seipsa, sit futura, tamen secundum modum cog-
noscentis est praesens; et ideo magis esset dicendum: Si Deus scit aliquid, illud
est; quam: hoc erit" *de Verit.* 2, 12, ad 7, in *Quaestiones Disputatae* (Turin: Marietti, 1953) 1:55.

[18]Thomas maintains later that they are determined by God as first cause.
Cf. 1a. 19, 8; 1a. 22, 2.

[19]If my interpretation of Thomas's reply to Argument A is correct, his position appears to depend on a libertarian view of human freedom. Thomas concludes that contingent events, including human free actions, cannot be
determined by divine knowledge as a prior condition. This is precisely what the
libertarian claims regarding all prior conditions of a free act: ". . . under the con-

future events, since all events are eternally *present* to the divine gaze. As a consequence, divine knowledge does not render its objects necessary.

In order to evaluate Thomas's reply to Argument A, some understanding of his conceptions of time and eternity is necessary. Thomas adopts Aristotle's account of time as "the numbering of before and after in change"[20] and Boethius's account of eternity as "the instantaneously whole and perfect possession of unending life."[21] Time, then, is the measure of change and succession, while eternity is the measure of an immutable and instantaneous whole.[22] God's eternal present contains the whole of time; in contrast, successive temporal presents each contain only a brief moment. The divine existence is eternal rather than temporal because it does not contain this succession of events that is for Thomas the essential characteristic of time.

Due perhaps to the fact that time and eternity are distinguished on the basis of the presence or absence of *succession*, the *Summa Theologiae* never clearly addresses the further question whether divine eternity is a kind of duration—a mode of existence which, although it is not marked by any internal change or succession, can nevertheless coexist with temporal succession.[23] Inter-

---

ditions then and theretofore prevailing, [the agent] was able to perform that act *and* he was also able to refrain from performing it." Richard Taylor, "Prevention, Postvention and the Will," in *Freedom and Determinism*, ed. Keith Lehrer (New York: Random House, 1966) 83.

[20]"Numerus motus secundum prius et posterius" 1a. 10, 1c (B 2:136). Cf. Aristotle, *Physics* 4, 11, 220a25.

[21]"Aeternitas est interminabilis vitae tota simul et perfecta possessio" 1a. 10, 1, 1 (B 2:134). Cf. Boethius, *de Consolatione* 5, prosa 6.

[22]"Aeternitas est mensura esse permanentis, tempus vero est mensura motus" 1a. 10, 4c (B 2:144).

[23]Eternity is held up as a sort of duration in objections at 1a. 10, 1, 2 & 6 (B 2:134): "aeternitas durationem quamdam significat." Thomas, however, does not unequivocally accept this claim in his reply to either objection. In response to a similar objection at 1a. 10, 4, 1, Thomas replies that eternity and time do not belong to the same genus, that is, the genus of duration, since they measure different kinds of things. These seem to be the only passages in the *Summa Theologiae* that directly relate eternity and duration.

preting divine eternity as unending duration would imply that God sees the whole of time *at all times.* In the *Summa contra Gentiles*, Thomas seems explicitly to accept a "durational" conception of eternity—'eternity' and 'sempiternity', or "existence at all times," are used interchangeably in several passages.[24] Perhaps, then, the vagueness of the *Summa Theologiae* on this issue represents an effort on Thomas's part to abandon this durational conception of eternity, even though he seems to have no clear alternative to offer. Thomas's reply to Argument A suggests one reason why he might have been dissatisfied with a durational conception of eternity, namely, that conception would reintroduce a sense of divine foreknowledge. If at all times God's knowledge includes everything in time, then God knows events before their occurrence in the world. Though such events are always present to God, they are future from the perspective of time.

Paul Helm has examined this relationship between divine knowledge and worldly events in a recent essay.[25] Helm argues that God's knowledge can be viewed as timeless (or durationless) from the divine perspective, but contends that the concept of foreknowledge still has an application, "not to a timeless knower's knowledge of certain events or actions, but to a temporal agent's *recognition* of timeless knowledge."[26] Although it would be impossible for a timeless knower to claim truly "I foreknow that x," where x is a future event, Helm argues that it is possible for a temporal agent truly to claim "He foreknows that x," where "He" refers to the timeless knower. This latter claim Helm paraphrases as follows:

(i) At a time before this time (the time of [i]'s utterance) the statement

---

[24]Cf. *Cont. Gent.* 1, 15 (Marietti, 1934) 1:15, 16: "quod semper fuit, habet virtutem semper essendi. Est igitur aeternus." Also, "prima autem substantia movens Deus est. Est igitur sempiternus." Also, *Cont. Gent.* 1, 99 (Marietti 1:90): "Igitur eius vita non habet successionem, sed est *tota simul.* Est igitur sempiterna."

[25]"Timelessness and Foreknowledge," *Mind* 84 (1975): 516-27.

[26]Ibid., 524.

"*T* timelessly knows *A*" (where *T* refers to the timeless knower, and *A* is an event future to the time of the statement's utterance) is true.[27]

In other words, Helm, like Thomas, rejects the expression used in Argument A, "God knew that *x* will happen," since this expression ascribes temporal status directly to God's knowledge. However, Helm accepts the expression " 'God knows (timelessly) that *x* happens at T2' is true at T1." This latter expression can substitute for the former expression in Argument A, since it establishes that God has knowledge of *x* before *x*'s occurrence in the world (premise [3]) and it entails that *x* will happen at T2 (premise [2]). Therefore, the conclusion Thomas wishes to deny, namely that the event *x* is necessary, appears to follow despite the fact that God's knowledge of *x* is eternally (timelessly) present. Helm states this conclusion as follows:

> If it is proper to speak of God's knowledge in this timeless way, then from the point in time of the temporal agent God knows beforehand. If he knows beforehand then it was true yesterday that God knows p. But this knowledge is past, and hence unchangeable, and so necessary. What it entails, the action that is foreknown, is likewise necessary. Hence there cannot be free will, even if God's knowledge of human actions is timeless.[28]

Thus the durational conception of eternity applied to divine knowledge results in a doctrine of theological determinism. God's complete knowledge of the world at all times becomes a prior condition to which all events must strictly correspond. This conclusion, though, contradicts Thomas's reply to Argument A. As Helm points out, it also denies human freedom, at least in the libertarian sense whereby freedom implies a choice between at least two genuinely open alternatives.

Insofar as it implies divine foreknowledge, and hence divine determinism, the durational conception of eternity does not seem

---

[27]Ibid., 525.

[28]Ibid., 527.

to be reconcilable with Thomas's reply to Argument A.[29] There still remain two possible accounts of divine omniscience that avoid ascribing foreknowledge to God and hence are not obviously vulnerable to Argument A. First, one could accept a durational conception of the divine eternity, but deny that God has foreknowledge of all future events, maintaining instead that God comes to know contingent future events only as they occur. This alternative was not open to Thomas, since it implies the existence of change and succession in the divine knowledge as God comes to know new events. It would, therefore, conflict with Thomas's explicit denial of change in God or in the divine knowledge.[30] This first account is Hartshorne's way of reconciling divine omniscience and human freedom. (Hartshorne's position will be outlined later in this chapter.)

Second, one could reject the durational conception of eternity in favor of a strictly timeless conception. That is, one may deny both temporal succession and temporal duration in God. According to this view, God exists "outside of time"; therefore, he bears no temporal relation to anything. In contrast to Helm's interpretation of timeless knowledge, this view would not permit temporal

---

[29]There is a good deal of evidence elsewhere in the *Summa Theologiae* to suggest that this reply may not be Thomas's last word on the relation between divine omniscience and human free will. For instance, Thomas speaks of the divine knowledge, in conjunction with the divine will, as the *cause* of all things (cf. 1a. 14, 8c & 11c). This notion of divine knowledge as causal provides an explanation for the relationship between events as they exist in the mind of God and events as they exist in the world, an explanation that is lacking in Thomas's reply to Argument A.

Thomas also acknowledges that divine will imparts a conditional necessity to events, but argues that this does not destroy their contingency (cf. 1a. 19, 8; 1a. 22, 4). The contingency of events, therefore, is based on the *kind* of *proximate* cause prepared for them, and is compatible with the fact that God is the first cause of all things. Thomas might wish to argue in parallel fashion that a divine *knowledge* of everlasting *duration* imparts conditional necessity to events, but does not destroy their contingency.

Such a compatibilist approach to the problem of reconciling omniscience and free will has its own difficulties, however. It appears, for example, to make God the ultimate cause of sinful acts. It will be considered at length in the section "The Compatibilist Alternative" later in this chapter, 21-27.

[30]1a. 9, 1; 1a. 14, 15.

agents to claim that "God knows x" is true at a particular time. This alternative is at least *prima facie* compatible with Thomas's doctrine of God. In fact, timelessness in this sense entails another divine attribute, immutability.[31] It also provides support for Thomas's doctrines of divine transcendence (since the mode of divine existence is fundamentally different from that of the world) and divine perfection (since God is not bound by the limits of time). Nelson Pike argues that this conception of eternity as strict timelessness is contained in Thomas's own explication of Boethius's definition of eternity at 1a. 10, 1.[32] Similarly, Anthony Kenny argues that a conception of eternity as "outside of time" is the key to Thomas's solution to Argument A.[33] Only the interpretation of eternity as timelessness, therefore, appears to be compatible with both Thomas's reply to Argument A and his doctrine of divine immutability.

A CONTEMPORARY VERSION OF THE ARGUMENT

In an essay entitled "Divine Omniscience and Voluntary Action"[34] and again in his book *God and Timelessness*,[35] Nelson Pike offers a reply similar to Thomas's to his own version of an argument asserting the incompatibility of foreknowledge and free will. Pike, however, comes to the explicit conclusion that God's knowledge must be held to be strictly timeless if it is to be compatible with human freedom. Unlike Thomas, Pike does not claim that divine knowledge bears a causal relationship to what is known.[36] In this way, he avoids two possible difficulties: (1) he is

---

[31] In order to change, an object must exist at two moments in time. Cf. Nelson Pike, *God and Timelessness* (New York: Schocken Books, 1970) 39.

[32] Ibid., 10.

[33] Anthony Kenny, "Divine Foreknowledge and Human Freedom," in *Aquinas*, ed. Anthony Kenny (London: Macmillan, 1969) 261-64. Kenny argues that Thomas's solution amounts to a denial of divine foreknowledge, 263.

[34] *Philosophical Review* 74 (1965): 27-46.

[35] Cf. n. 31 above.

[36] *God and Timelessness*, 64.

not committed to the view that divine knowledge causally determines human actions, and (2) he is not required to explain how a timeless cause can bring about temporal effects. (Consequently, in his explanation of divine knowledge, Pike abandons Thomas's example of an artist, a knower who creates the objects of his knowledge, in favor of the example of an infallible crystal-ball gazer.[37])

Let us consider Pike's formulation of the argument from divine foreknowledge against free will. Pike states the argument (henceforward called Argument B) as follows:

(1') "Yahweh is omniscient and Yahweh exists at T1" entails "If Jones does A at T2, then Yahweh believes at T1 that Jones does A at T2."

(2') If Yahweh is (essentially) omniscient, then "Yahweh believes P" entails "P."

(3') It is not within one's power at a given time so to act that both "P" and "not-P" are true.

(4') It is not within one's power at a given time so to act that something believed by an individual at a time prior to the given time was not believed by that individual at the prior time.

(5') It is not within one's power at a given time so to act that an individual existing at a time prior to the given time did not exist at the prior time.

(6') If Yahweh believes at T1 that Jones does A at T2, then if it is within Jones's power at T2 to refrain from doing A, then either: (1) It was within Jones's power at T2 so to act that Yahweh believed P at T1 and "P" is false; or (2) it was within Jones's power at T2 so to act that Yahweh did not believe as he did believe at T2; or (3) it was within Jones's power at T2 so to act that Yahweh did not exist at T1.

(7') If Yahweh is (essentially) omniscient, then the first alternative in the consequent of line 6' is false (from lines 2' and 3').

(8') The second alternative in the consequent of line 6' is false (from line 4').

(9') The third alternative in the consequent of line 6' is false (from line 5').

(10') Therefore: If Yahweh is (essentially) omniscient and believes at T1 that Jones does A at T2, then it was not within Jones' power at T2 to refrain from doing A (from lines 6' and 7'-9').

(11') Therefore: If Yahweh is (essentially) omniscient and exists at T1,

---

[37]Ibid., 55.

then if Jones does A at T2, it was not within Jones' power at T2 to refrain from doing A (from lines 10' and 1').[38]

Argument B differs from Thomas's Agrument A in several ways that merit closer examination. First, we should note that premise (2') plays the same role in Pike's argument that premise (2) plays in Thomas's—both establish the claim that "God knows (or believes) p" entails "p." (Pike's argument, however, remains conditional while Argument A adopts a categorical form.[39]) The justification offered for the claim that "God knows p" entails "p," however, is different in the two arguments. Thomas appeals to the logic of the term 'know', contending that "knowledge is only of what is true." In contrast, Pike adopts a much weaker sense of the term 'know'. He identifies knowledge with correct belief, that is, belief that turns out to be true.[40] Pike maintains that in the ordinary case of foreknowledge, only material implication holds between the statements "X knows p" and "p is true."

> If we suppose that Smith *knew* at T1 that Jones does A at T2 , what we are supposing is that Smith believed at T1 that Jones does A at T2 and, *as an additional contingent fact*, that the belief held by Smith at T1 was true.[41]

Since the consequent "p is true" is merely "an additional contingent fact," the conditional is not an instance of entailment. Pike holds, nevertheless, that in the case of *divine* foreknowledge, "God knows that p" does entail "p." This special claim is based on Pike's doctrine of essential omniscience. This doctrine consists in the following two claims: (1) "God is omniscient" is a necessary statement; and (2) Omniscience is an essential or necessary prop-

---

[38]Ibid., 59-60. (In this statement of the argument, Pike uses the term 'Yahweh' as the proper name of the supreme being. He distinguishes it from the term 'God', which he uses as a title-term.)

[39]In his earlier statement of this argument (in "Divine Omniscience and Voluntary Action," 33-34), Pike also adopts a categorical formulation. The change in this later statement is apparently intended to make the dependence of the argument on the doctrine of essential omniscience more obvious.

[40]*God and Timelessness*, 79.

[41]Ibid., (italics in original).

erty of any individual who possesses it. Together, these two claims imply that it is conceptually impossible for the individual who is God to hold a false belief, that is "Yahweh believes p" entails "p."[42]

The special assumption of essential omniscience in God is, then, required in Pike's argument in order to strengthen the rather weak general implications of knowledge instances as Pike interprets them. Pike suggests that Augustine avoids the deterministic conclusion of Argument B by denying this strong sense of omniscience.[43] It seems clear, however, that Thomas does commit himself to the doctrine of essential omniscience or to something very similar in his claim that God's "act of knowing is his essence and his being."[44] Thus we may appeal to Thomas's acceptance of the doctrine of essential omniscience to bolster premise (2).

We may also argue that premise (2) has adequate justification in the logic of the term 'know' and does not require the strong additional assumption of essential omniscience.[45] That is, we may challenge Pike's analysis of the term 'know'. For instance, on Pike's account, it would seem that one could not justifiably assert at T1 that a (nondivine) person X knew at T1 that an event e would occur at T2, *until* the event did in fact occur and hence X's belief turned out to be true. Rather, all one could assert at T1 would be that X believes e will occur at T2. In other words, one could only make retrospective claims about foreknowledge, such

---

[42]Ibid., 54-56.

[43]Ibid., 83.

[44]"Ex necessitate sequitur quod ipsum ejus intelligere sit ejus essentia et ejus esse" 1a. 14, 4c (B 4:16).

[45]In other discussions of this argument, Cahn, Helm, Kane, Kenny, and Plantinga all accept Thomas's claim that "X knows p" entails "p is true." See Steven M. Cahn, *Fate, Logic, and Time* (New Haven: Yale University Press, 1967) 75; Paul Helm, "Divine Foreknowledge and Facts," *Canadian Journal of Philosophy* 4 (1974): 309; R. H. Kane, "Divine Foreknowledge and Causal Determinism," *Southwestern Journal of Philosophy* 9 (1978): 73; Kenny, "Divine Foreknowledge and Human Freedom," 265; and Alvin Plantinga, *God, Freedom, and Evil* (New York: Harper & Row, 1974) 67.

as a claim at T3 that X had foreknowledge at T1 that e would occur at T2 (that is, a claim made after e has occurred).

In order to be justified at T1 in making the stronger claim that *X knows at T1* that e will occur at T2, there must be a relation stronger than that of two successive but logically independent contingent facts between X's belief at T1 that e will occur and the occurrence of e at T2. Pike's argument seems to imply that human beings are never justified in making present-tense claims of foreknowledge, since only the occurrence of the event determines whether the belief is true or not. Pike does, however, make present-tense claims about human foreknowledge, as in the following passage.

> When my wife is in the throes of decision as to which of two kinds of pie to buy for supper, I know how she is going to choose. There is only one kind of pie we like; she always buys apple. But, surely my wife chooses apple of her own free will. The fact that I know how she is going to choose before the decision is made does nothing to diminish this fact.[46]

Given his claim that knowledge is belief that turns out to be true, in this case all Pike seems justified in asserting (before his wife's choice) is that he believes his wife will choose apple. Whether his belief is true (and can therefore be called 'knowledge') will be determined by the choice his wife does in fact make.

Perhaps what Pike is suggesting in the above example is that his knowledge of the causal conditions in this situation (e.g., his wife's habits, her perception of the family's desires) is such that she cannot fail to choose apple, though her choice remains free. In that case, Mrs. Pike's decision might be called free in the compatibilist sense that she is under no external constraint, though it is obviously not free in the libertarian sense of a choice among really possible alternatives. This interpretation, however, simply replaces the knowledge-object entailment relation Pike denies with a cause-effect entailment relation. Furthermore, as we will observe later,[47] Pike explicitly rejects a compatibilist interpretation

---

[46]*God and Timelessness*, 77.

[47]See section on "Plantinga's Reply" in this chapter, 18-21.

of freedom for Argument B. In sum, then, Thomas's claim that "God knows p" entails "p"—premise (2) of Argument A—does not seem to require Pike's additional assumption of a doctrine of God's "essential omniscience," though acceptance of that doctrine would provide additional support for the above claim.

The second major difference between Argument A and Argument B is quite obvious. While Thomas's argument is couched in terms of the necessity of an event, Pike's argument focuses on what it is within one's power at a given time to do. Pike points out that the term 'necessity' in traditional formulations of this problem, like that of Augustine, does not mean logical necessity, but a sense of necessity that contrasts with the term 'voluntary'.[48] Pike's own argument, therefore, expresses this sense of necessity in terms of what it is and is not within one's power at a given time to do. We have already noted that the sense of necessity at work in much of Argument A is not logical necessity. Since both arguments reach the same conclusion as regards the freedom of human actions, and since both rely on the claim that "God knows p" entails "p," the form of the argument in B may help us to elucidate the sense of necessity involved in Argument A.

Argument B assumes that if an action A is free, it must be within one's power to refrain from A. But power to refrain from an action foreknown by God would be power so to act that either: (1) God's knowledge (belief) is false, or (2) God did not believe what he (by hypothesis) did believe at T1, or (3) God did not exist at T1. None of these alternatives, it is argued, is within one's power—alternative (1) because it implies a contradiction, and alternatives (2) and (3) because they imply that the past be different in particular ways (by not containing either God's belief at T1 or God himself at T1). If this argument is sound, then action A is not free; it is a necessary as opposed to a voluntary action. This conclusion is clearly dependent on the claim that persons are not able so to act that the past be different. In this way Argument B makes ex-

---

[48]Pike's comment on Augustine is based on a passage in *De Libero Arbitrio* 3,3. Steven Cahn characterizes the sort of necessity involved here as follows: "An event is necessary if no man can prevent its occurrence." (*Fate, Logic, and Time*, 70).

plicit the connection between necessary in the sense of involuntary and necessary in the sense of now past as attributed to God's knowledge in Argument A. We may therefore view Argument B as focusing the conclusion of Argument A on the case of human action.

Both Arguments A and B clearly depend on the assumption of divine foreknowledge, that is, the location of God's knowledge in time prior to the event or action known. Only in this way can the events in question be bound by the irrevocability of the past. Like Thomas, then, Pike avers that the conclusion, "all events are necessary," may be avoided by denying that God's knowledge can be located in the past relative to its objects. Pike recognizes more clearly than Thomas that the way to avoid foreknowledge without compromising the immutability of divine knowledge is to hold that it is strictly timeless, that is, without temporal duration or location.[49]

PLANTINGA'S REPLY

In his book *God, Freedom, and Evil*,[50] Alvin Plantinga contends against Pike that Argument B does not show the incompatibility of divine omniscience and human freedom. Plantinga accepts the two assumptions of Argument B Pike finds most vulnerable, that is, God's essential omniscience and the location of divine knowledge in the past relative to its objects. Plantinga then attempts to clarify Argument B by interpreting it in terms of the logical apparatus of possible-worlds ontology. He focuses on the complex premise (6'). Using the language of possible worlds, he interprets the claim that it is in Jones's power to refrain from A as equivalent to the claim that there is a possible world W in which Jones does refrain from A at T2.[51] If Jones's power to refrain from A is interpreted in this way, Plantinga argues, it does not follow that Jones has the power to act so that God held a false belief at

---

[49]*God and Timelessness*, 74-75.

[50]*God, Freedom and Evil*, 67-73.

[51]Ibid., 70-71.

T1, as alternative (1) of premise (6') asserts; for in W, God does not believe (falsely) at T1 that Jones will do A at T2. Rather, in W God believes (truly) that Jones will refrain from A at T2. Plantinga therefore analyzes Jones's power as power so to act that a belief God did hold at T1 *would have been* false.

Likewise, Plantinga interprets alternative (2) of premise (6'), Jones's power so to act that God did not believe he would do A at T2, as the existence of a possible world W in which Jones refrains from A at T2 and God does not believe at T1 that Jones will do A at T2. Alternative (3) of premise (6') is treated similarly by denying that in W God holds the false belief that Jones would do A at T2. Since Plantinga finds no difficulty in affirming the existence of a possible world in which Jones's actions and God's beliefs differ from their counterparts in the actual world, he concludes that Jones retains the power to choose his actions and that Argument B does not demonstrate the incompatibility of divine foreknowledge and human freedom.

As Plantinga points out elsewhere in his book,[52] the language of possible worlds is used to elucidate the notions of logical possibility, impossibility, and necessity. As noted, however, Arguments A and B are not concerned solely with logical necessity but also with senses of necessity related to pastness and lack of freedom. This suggests that Plantinga's translation of Argument B into the idiom of possible worlds may not capture the proper sense of the modal notions involved. In fact, Plantinga's criticism of Argument B has recently been challenged on these grounds by Pike.[53]

Pike argues that Plantinga conflates the notion of what it is within one's power to do with the notion of what it is logically possible for one to do. What it is within one's power to do, Pike argues, designates a much narrower range of actions than what it is logically possible for one to do. The former, but not the latter set of actions, is circumscribed by a number of conditions that obtain in

---

[52]Ibid., 37.

[53]Nelson Pike, "Divine Foreknowledge, Human Freedom, and Possible Worlds," *Philosophical Review* 86 (1977): 209-16.

the actual world, including what happened in the past relative to the time in question. Whether it is within my power to do *A* at T2, Pike argues, depends not on whether I do *A* in any possible world, but upon whether I do *A* in some possible world "having a history prior to T2 that is indistinguishable from that of the actual world."[54] If, therefore, God believes at T1 that Jones does *A* at T2, there is no possible world sharing the history of the actual world in which Jones refrains from doing *A* at T2. Hence Pike stands by his conclusion that the set of assumptions articulated in Argument B entail that no human action is free.

Although it is never stated as a premise of Argument B, Pike's reply to Plantinga clearly indicates that the conception of freedom implied by Argument B is a libertarian one. Pike's account of freedom in terms of possible worlds with indistinguishable histories is equivalent to the libertarian conception of freedom as the ability, all conditions remaining the same, to either perform or refrain from performing a particular action *A*.[55] While Pike is clearly correct in arguing that Plantinga's identification of the power to do *A* with the logical possibility that one do *A* includes too *broad* a range of actions within one's power, Pike's own analysis seems vulnerable to the objection that it is too *narrow*.

The compatibilist, for example, is clearly committed to denying that an action is free only if, given all prior conditions, two alternatives are (physically) possible.[56] Thus, in response to Pike, John Turk Saunders argues that one's power to do *A* at T2 depends merely on one's knowing how to do *A* and the existence of "normal conditions" at T2 (that is, a situation in which one has not been

---

[54]Ibid., 216.

[55]Cf. D. J. O'Connor, *Free Will* (Garden City NY: Doubleday, 1971) 82.

[56]Compatibilism receives its name from the belief that freedom is compatible with universal causal determinism. This theory is based on a distinction between actions that are caused and actions that are compelled. Actions are free as long as they are based on one's desires and inclinations, despite the fact that these desires and inclinations have their own causal history. Actions are not free when they are constrained or coerced, caused by forces that conflict with one's desires and inclinations.

"hypnotized, drugged, threatened, manhandled, and so forth").[57] Cast in the language of possible worlds, this notion of power may be analyzed as follows:

> Within the subset of possible worlds having the following conditions indistinguishable from those of the actual world prior to T2: (C1) The state of one's "know-how" regarding A, and (C2) The presence or absence of direct mental or physical constraint on one's performance of A, there is a possible world in which one does A at T2.

On this account, only *some* conditions present in the actual world are relevant to the assertion that one has the power to do A; other conditions, therefore, need *not* be the same as in the actual world. Saunders offers an example of a case in which power to do A implies that a particular prior condition, namely a past decision to do B, would be other than it is. Based on this analysis and example, he maintains that one may have the power so to act that something in the past would be other than it is, and hence he rejects premises (4') and (5') of Argument B.

Saunders is, I believe, correct in arguing that a compatibilist conception of power does imply that one has the power so to act that the past would be other than it is. Pike may reply that this implication suggests the inadequacy of the compatibilist conception of power. In any case, it seems clear that the cogency of Argument B depends on the presupposition or the independent demonstration of a libertarian conception of freedom.

THE COMPATIBILIST ALTERNATIVE

In the first sections of this chapter, our discussion of the problem of reconciling divine knowledge and human freedom concentrated on which of several interpretations of omniscience is compatible with the implicitly libertarian doctrine of freedom contained in Arguments A and B. The Plantinga-Pike-Saunders exchange considered in the previous section adds another dimen-

---

[57]John Turk Saunders, "Of God and Freedom," *Philosophical Review* 75 (1966): 219-25. By "normal conditions," Saunders seems to mean the absence of direct interference in one's decision-making process (as in hypnotism) or in one's ability to act on one's decisions (as in physical restraint).

sion to this discussion by demonstrating that there is at least one clear alternative to a libertarian conception of freedom, namely the compatibilist conception proposed by Saunders. In fact, just as Pike is able to reconcile a timeless divine knowledge with libertarian freedom, so is the compatibilist position able to reconcile an everlasting divine knowledge (including divine foreknowledge) with its own conception of freedom.

Indeed, there are good grounds for holding that the compatibilist answer to this problem is the predominant view among classical theologians. This position seems to be dictated, for instance, by the doctrines of creation, providence, grace, and predestination, all of which are affirmed by Thomas. Creation signifies in this context that God is the cause of all existing things.[58] By his providence God establishes and maintains the order of the universe in every detail.[59] The clear emphasis in these doctrines is on the divine power in establishing and ordering the universe; they do not provide for activity outside the scope of the divine power. The relation of the divine providence to human beings is specified in the doctrines of grace and predestination. By grace God calls those whom he wishes to be saved and allows others to be damned. Although it is necessary for salvation, this calling cannot be merited; it is strictly a matter of divine choice.[60] Since these doctrines strongly suggest a divine determinism, only a compatibilist conception of freedom would seem to be consistent with them. Augustine, for instance, articulates a clearly compatibilist conception of free will.[61]

Despite the fact that compatibilism does appear to be the predominant solution to the problem of reconciling divine activity and human free will in classical theology, I do not intend to pursue it further in this essay. I have two major reasons for preferring to

---

[58] 1a. 44, 1.

[59] 1a. 22, 2.

[60] 1a. 23, 5.

[61] See Augustine, *Retractations*, in *On Free Choice of the Will* (Indianapolis: Bobbs-Merrill, 1964) 155-58.

work instead with the libertarian view. First, despite the above passages, I believe that Thomas himself is not entirely consistent in his account of free will. As has been noted earlier, Thomas's reply to Argument A depends on the denial that God's knowledge is a *prior* condition of contingent events—a reply whose intelligibility depends on the underlying libertarian assumption that an action cannot be free if it has been determined by antecedent conditions.

Thomas's explication of the concept of free will (*liberum arbitrium*) also seems much closer to the libertarian than to the compatibilist conception of freedom. While the compatibilist bases freedom on the power to act as one wills (though the will itself may be determined), Thomas stresses the claim that with regard to particular actions, "judgment is open to various possibilities, not determined to one."[62] Thomas does add that God is the first cause of free action, but the way in which divine and human initiatives interact is not further elaborated.[63]

In addition to these suggestive passages in Thomas, I wish to work with a libertarian doctrine rather than the traditional compatibilist theology because there appear to be serious weaknesses in the traditional Augustinian explanations of the nature and amount of evil in the world. These weaknesses have been stressed by theistic and nontheistic philosophers alike.[64] To illustrate the most significant problems, let us now consider two basic themes of Augustinian theodicy, namely sin as the origin of evil and punishment as the response to sin. These two, sin and its punishment, exhaust the category of evil in Augustine's view: "omne quod dicitur malum, aut peccatum esse, aut poenam peccati."[65]

---

[62]"Et ideo circa ea judicium rationis ad diversa se habet, et non est determinatum ad unum. Et pro tanto necesse est quod homo sit liberi arbitrii, ex hoc ipso quod rationalis est" 1a. 83, 1c (B 11:238).

[63]1a., 83, 1 ad 3.

[64]See, e.g., John Hick, *Evil and the God of Love*, 2nd ed. (London: Macmillan, 1977) 38-114; and Edward H. Madden and Peter H. Hare, *Evil and the Concept of God* (Springfield IL: Charles C. Thomas, 1968) 52-82.

[65]Augustine, *De Genesi Ad Litteram*, cited in Hick, *Evil and the God of Love*, 59.

Central to Augustine's theodicy, and to that of most Christian theologians after him, is the claim that evil originates in the misuse of creaturely free will.[66] If evil is solely the product of free will, then it can be ascribed neither to God (except in his activity of punishing sinners) nor to his creation. Despite its popularity, however, this freewill defense of God's goodness does not appear to be easily reconciled with a deterministic theology like that of Augustine.

If God's creation is wholly good, then the decision of angels or of men to sin seems incomprehensible. Why, for instance, should an angel will to turn away from God, the source of its good? Augustine answers that this is due to the vice of pride.[67] But then this pride must itself be either the result of a choice made by the angel, or a part of the angel's nature as created by God. If we embrace the first alternative, we are faced with the mysterious decision of an uncorrupted creature to do evil. Hick calls this "the incomprehensible conception of the self-creation of evil *ex nihilo*."[68] If, however, we choose the second alternative, it seems that creation can no longer be said to be wholly good, since it already contains a disposition of creatures to commit sin.

In fact, Augustine himself appears to have adopted a version of the second alternative, for he claims that the fidelity of the angels depends upon the amount of grace each receives.[69] Yet with this doctrine, Augustine's position shifts from emphasis on angelic self-determination to divine preordination of angelic will and action. A similar emphasis on the divine predestination of human beings is evident in Augustine's late treatises against the Pe-

---

[66] Augustine, *De Libero Arbitrio*, trans. Anna S. Benjamin and L. H. Hackstaff (Indianapolis: Bobbs Merrill, 1964) bk. 1, ch. 1.

[67] Augustine, *De Civitate Dei*, trans. Marcus Dods (New York: Modern Library, 1950) bk. 12, ch. 6.

[68] Hick, *Evil and the God of Love*, 66.

[69] Augustine, *De Civitate Dei*, 12, 9.

lagians.[70] The doctrine of predestination, however, is even more damaging to a freewill defense than the incomprehensibility of a good creature's choice of evil. If God is the ultimate cause of human actions, then God clearly cannot be absolved of all responsibility for the evil that people do. Rather, he must at least share responsibility for evil with his creatures.

Thomas, it is true, argues that God does not directly will the sins of human beings, but rather *permits* them to occur.[71] Thomas also holds, however, that the question of whether a person sins or does not sin is solely dependent on being given God's gift of grace.[72] But if this is the case, the presence or absence of evil remains in God's hands no matter whether his action is called 'willing' or 'permitting'. Even supposing God is not the direct cause of a person's sin, he still plays a role in the origin of evil if he creates individuals with the knowledge that they will sin. If God chose to make creatures who he knows will sin, perhaps he should not take offense when they do sin. Furthermore, as was already noted, Thomas's own reply to Argument A suggests that divine foreknowledge would, in fact, conflict with human freedom. Despite the prominence of the freewill defense in Christian theodicy, then, its strength as an explanation of the origin of evil is largely vitiated by the traditional doctrines of providence, predestination, and foreknowledge.

Let us turn now to a second theme of the traditional theodicy, the view that human suffering is ordained by God as punishment for sin. This punishment is thought to be a necessary measure for

---

[70]The following passage is an example: "Therefore God chose us in Christ before the foundation of the world, predestinating us to the adoption of children, not because we were going to be of ourselves holy and immaculate, but He chose and predestinated us that we might be so." "On the Predestination of the Saints," trans. Peter Holmes and Robert E. Wallis, in *Saint Augustine: Anti-Pelagian Writings*, ed. Philip Schaff, Library of the Nicene and Post-Nicene Fathers, Vol. 5 (New York: Christian Literature Co., 1887) 516.

[71]1a. 19, 9 ad 3.

[72]1a2ae. 109, 5; 1a2ae. 109, 8.

restoring the moral balance of the universe when it is violated by sin.

> Punishment is used in such a way that it places natures in their right order (that is, where it is not a disgrace for them to be) and forces them to comply with the beauty of the universe, so that the punishment of sin corrects the disgrace of sin.[73]

Underlying this view of punishment is the belief that God appreciates the universe as an aesthetic harmony, disturbed by sin but immediately restored by punishment.

There are several basic objections to this doctrine. First, punishment for sins is not justified unless the sinner bears responsibility for his actions. As noted earlier, however, the deterministic doctrines of traditional theology vitiate the claim that individuals are responsible for their sinful acts. Even if creaturely responsibility for sin is granted, it seems impossible that the actual distribution of suffering in the world is the result of God's punishment of sinners. Suffering often afflicts the relatively innocent, particularly children, while evil individuals flourish. The traditional reply to this criticism is that some suffering is a consequence of original sin.[74] If true, the meaning and significance of original sin must then be explained. Original sin will not be a very satisfying justification for divine punishment if it requires us to accept the story of Adam's fall as a historical fact the consequences of which we still experience or if it fails to explain why God should punish Adam's descendants for their father's sin.

Perhaps the most serious objection to the doctrine of suffering as punishment for sin concerns the idea of divine justice. This doctrine appeals to divine justice in exacting a retribution that restores the ultimate harmony of the universe by punishing the sinful. But it ignores the fact that in the traditional view, all human beings share a more fundamental equality; that is, all are created as manifestations of divine love and all are completely de-

---

[73]Augustine, *De Libero Arbitrio*, bk. 3, ch. 9.

[74]Charles Journet, *The Meaning of Evil*, trans. Michael Barry (London: Geoffrey Chapman, 1963) 218.

pendent on divine grace for salvation. Given this fundamental
equality of persons, it appears that the divine decision that some
will be saved and others damned must be purely arbitrary. How,
then, can this be a just sentence for those condemned to eternal
torment?

Finally, the doctrine of the necessity of punishment suggests
a view of man as the occupant of a small niche in the cosmic hi-
erarchy. Human suffering, even eternal suffering, can therefore be
accepted as necessary for the aesthetic harmony of the whole. This
emphasis on the universe as a whole, however, leaves little room
for the notion of a personal and loving relationship between God
and individual persons. Based on his analysis of this and other
doctrines, Hick concludes that "the central stream of the Augustinian theodicy tradition operates within a framework that is seriously inadequate for the consideration of God's relationship to
His creation as this has been revealed to us in the person and work
of Jesus Christ."[75]

I propose, then, to consider Thomas's doctrine of God in relation to the libertarian framework suggested by Pike rather than
the traditional compatibilist theology. Though my approach is
surely more modern than medieval, I believe that there are hints
of the doctrines of timelessness and libertarianism in Thomas
himself. Even if only in view of the adherence of many modern
theologians and philosophers to the libertarian position, it will be
useful to consider whether that position is compatible with Thomas's doctrine of God. The next two chapters will examine the relation of a doctrine of divine timelessness to Thomas's accounts of
divine knowledge and will.

HARTSHORNE
AND DIVINE RELATIVITY

As was observed in the discussion of Aquinas and Pike, divine
omniscience and human freedom may be reconciled by removing
God from the sphere of temporality and thereby denying any temporal relation between divine knowledge and human action. In

---

[75]Hick, *Evil and the God of Love*, 195-96.

sharp contrast to this solution to the problem, an approach proposed by Charles Hartshorne[76] places God unequivocally in time,
adds to the temporal a causal relation between divine knowledge
and human action, and makes human action temporally and
causally *prior* to divine knowledge of that action. The two approaches do have one important feature in common: both deny
that God knows *beforehand* what a person will do of his own free
will. Thus neither position is obviously vulnerable to Arguments
A and B. In order to deny foreknowledge of free actions while affirming God's existence in time, Hartshorne abandons the immutability of divine knowledge and modifies the traditional
conception of omniscience.

Hartshorne contends that God comes to know human actions
(and other events) in experiencing them, and his all-pervasive
presence experiences each event as it occurs. His knowledge is cumulative; it continuously experiences new actions and events
while retaining all previous experiences.[77] Thus, for Hartshorne,
God knows both the present as present and the past as past in
their complete particularity; he knows the future as future, that
is, as partially indefinite and undetermined. This, Hartshorne
claims, is the ideal of knowledge, since it alone completely and accurately reflects the unfolding of events in time. The fact that God
does not have completely determinate knowledge of the future is
not, Hartshorne contends, an imperfection, for the free aspects of
the future are in principle not knowable in advance.

This, in brief outline, is the second solution to the problem of
reconciling divine omniscience and human freedom we will consider. It will be examined at greater length in chapter four.

---

[76]Hartshorne's remarks on divine knowledge are dispersed throughout his
writings. See, for example, *The Divine Relativity* (New Haven: Yale University
Press, 1948) 8-15, and *Creative Synthesis and Philosophic Method* (LaSalle IL:
Open Court, 1970) ch. 11:227-43.

[77]Hartshorne, *Reality as Social Process* (Glencoe IL: Free Press, 1953) 41-42.

CHAPTER TWO

THE DOCTRINE
OF ETERNAL
KNOWLEDGE

C hapter one suggested a solution to the problem of reconciling divine omniscience and human freedom
based on a strict distinction between eternity, the mode of divine
existence, and time, the mode of human existence. Given this distinction, Aquinas and Pike are able to deny that God's knowledge
of human actions is *temporally* prior to the actions themselves. It
is now appropriate to examine more closely the conception of a
timelessly eternal God.

ETERNITY AND IMMUTABILITY

It has already been noted that Thomas defends Boethius's definition of eternity as "the simultaneously whole and perfect possession of unending life."[1] Thomas uses the phrase
'simultaneously whole' to assert the indivisibility of eternity and

---

[1] "... aeternitas est interminabilis vitae tota simul et perfecta possessio" 1a.
10, 1, 1 (B 2:134). Cf. Boethius, *de Consolatione* 5, prosa 6.

to distinguish eternity from time, which is successive and divisible into parts. The phrase 'perfect possession' is meant to distinguish the eternal "moment" from the fleeting, and hence imperfect, temporal moment.[2] In general, then, time reflects the successiveness of changing beings, while eternity is the mode of existence of the immutable, that which lacks successiveness and beginning or end. Eternity is, in fact, a mode of life, the immutable life of God and of those who share the beatific vision.[3]

Having characterized eternity as the mode of existence of the immutable, Thomas derives the *divine* eternity from the complete immutability of God.[4] Divine immutability, in turn, is based on the following three arguments:[5] (1) Thomas's first proof for the existence of God posits a sheerly actual first cause of all change.[6] Such a cause can possess no potentiality, but without potentiality, change is impossible. Hence God cannot change in any way. (2) Things undergoing change are always composite, that is, partly changing and partly persisting. But Thomas has already demonstrated that God is altogether simple,[7] and therefore he cannot change. (3) Thomas contends that change is the acquisition of something not previously possessed. God, however, already possesses the fullness of existence and cannot acquire anything new; as a result, God cannot change. In general, then, Thomas holds that change, or the actualization of a potential, is completely foreign to God.

---

[2]"... in tempore est duo considerare, scilicet ipsum tempus quod est successivum, et nunc temporis quod est imperfectum. Dicit ergo tota simul ad removendum tempus, et perfecta ad excludendum nunc temporis" 1a. 10, 1, ad 5 (B 2:136).

[3]1a. 10, 3.

[4]"Ratio aeternitatis consequitur immutabilitatem, sicut ratio temporis consequitur motum, ut ex dictis patet [cf. 1a. 10, 1]. Unde cum Deus sit maxime immutabilis sibi maxime competit esse aeternum" 1a. 10, 2 (B 2:138).

[5]1a. 9, 1c.

[6]1a. 2, 3c.

[7]1a. 3, 7c.

From his basic doctrine of divine immutability, Thomas concludes further that the divine activities of knowledge and will, because they are identical to the divine substance, are also immutable and eternal.[8] Thomas maintains that these activities in God (unlike their counterparts in humans) do not entail change because they do not involve movement from potentiality to actuality.[9] The rest of this chapter will review Thomas's account of God's eternal knowledge and then consider several criticisms of that account. Chapter three will then examine the corresponding account of divine will.

AQUINAS'S DOCTRINE OF OMNISCIENCE

Thomas begins his account of the divine knowledge by contrasting it with human knowledge. He notes that in the human act of knowing, the intellect receives the intellectual likeness (*species intelligibilis*) of an object. Prior to the act of knowing, both the intellect and the object are in potency: the intellect is a potential knower (it is able to know) and the object is potentially known (it is able to be known).[10]

For at least two reasons, Thomas cannot explain divine knowledge in this way. First, he has demonstrated that God is pure actuality, and he now concludes that for this reason the divine knowledge can contain no element of potentiality. Second, because God as first cause is completely independent and self-sufficient, his knowledge cannot be dependent on any external object.

---

[8] ". . . cum scientia Dei sit ejus substantia, ut ex dictis patet [1a. 14, 4], sicut substantia ejus est omnino immutabilis, ut supra ostensum est [1a. 9, 1], ita oportet scientiam ejus omnino invariabilem esse" 1a. 14, 15 (B 4:54). Also, ". . . tam substantia Dei quam ejus scientia est omnino immutabilis. Unde oportet voluntatem ejus omnino esse immutabilem" 1a. 19, 7c (B 5:32).

[9] 1a. 9, 1, ad 1.

[10] "Ex hoc enim aliquid in actu sentimus vel intelligimus, quod intellectus noster vel sensus informatur per speciem sensibilem vel intelligibilem. Et secundum hoc tantum sensus vel intellectus est aliud a sensibili vel intelligibili quia utrumque est in potentia" 1a. 14, 2c (B 4:8).

Like Aristotle, Thomas resolves these difficulties by claiming that in God, knower and known are identical in every way.[11] Unlike human knowers, God does not receive the form of something other than himself; rather, God's knowledge is knowledge of himself, and as such it is purely actual, complete, and self-sufficient. Thus the divine intellect, the object of divine knowledge, and the divine act of knowing are one and the same, and identical to the divine substance or essence.[12]

Contrary to Aristotle, Thomas claims that the fact that the object of God's knowledge is himself does not imply that God is ignorant of other things. Thomas bases this claim on an appeal to God's power as manifested in his creative activity. He argues that since God's knowledge of himself is his substance, the attributes of the divine being, including perfection, may be ascribed to it. But if God's knowledge of himself is perfect, it must include knowledge of the extent of his power. Because God's power extends to all beings as their first cause, and effects preexist in their causes, God knows all things in knowing himself.[13]

This conclusion would seem to reintroduce the above-mentioned difficulty of divine dependence on another, but Thomas argues that it does not. He points out that God does not receive his knowledge of nondivine things from the things themselves. Rather, God knows everything in himself since the likenesses of all things preexist in him as their first cause. Therefore, the divine knowledge of all things depends on the divine essence alone.[14] This solution suggests that a plurality of diverse ideas exists in the divine intellect, and in fact, Thomas acknowledges a

---

[11]"Cum igitur Deus nihil potentialitatis habeat, sed sit actus purus, oportet quod in eo intellectus et intellectum sint idem omnibus modis" 1a. 14, 2c (B 4:10).

[12]". . . in Deo intellectus, et id quod intelligitur, et species intelligibilis, et ipsum intelligere, sunt omnino unum et idem" 1a. 14, 4c (B 4:16).

[13]"Unde quicumque effectus praeexistunt in Deo sicut in causa prima, necesse est quod sint in ipso ejus intelligere" 1a. 14, 5c (B 4:18).

[14]". . . cum essentia Dei habeat in se quidquid perfectionis habet essentia cujuscunque rei alterius, et adhuc amplius, Deus in seipso potest omnia propria cognitione cognoscere" 1a. 14, 6c (B 4:24).

plurality of divine ideas. He claims at the same time that this is not inconsistent with the divine simplicity. The divine ideas arise out of God's knowledge of his essence as imitable in particular ways by particular creatures, and hence the divine essence remains the sole object of divine knowledge.[15]

Thomas goes on to consider the depth of God's knowledge of all things. Since God's knowledge is perfect and complete, it must include not only what all creatures have in common as beings, but also the specific nature and accidents of each. God possesses this knowledge because he is the cause not merely of the being of creatures, but also of all the diverse properties manifested both in species and in individuals. Thomas maintains that God knows all these things in an eternal, immutable unity, since he sees everything in one, that is, in his eternal, immutable self.[16]

As the artist's knowledge is the cause of his work of art, so also for Thomas is God's knowledge the cause of all created things. Divine knowledge can, however, be completely indifferent to the existence of an object, in which case nothing external results from that knowledge. Rather, in creating anything, God's knowledge of the thing is accompanied by an inclination to produce it, which is provided by his will. It is, therefore, God's knowledge of approbation that is the cause of all created things—including, Thomas later claims, the free actions of human beings.[17]

God has, in addition, knowledge of nonexistent things, namely all those things that could be produced by God or by creatures, but which do not actually exist. Here Thomas distinguishes between those things that do not now, but once did or will in the future exist, and those things that never did, do not now, and never will exist. The former God is said to know by knowledge of vision, for his

---

[15]"Sic igitur inquantum Deus cognoscit essentiam suam ut sic imitabilem a tali creatura, cognoscit eam ut propriam rationem et ideam hujus creaturae; et similiter de aliis" 1a. 15, 3c (B 4:68).

[16]"Deus autem omnia videt in uno, quod est ipse, ut habitum est [1a. 14, 5]. Unde simul et non successive omnia videt" 1a. 14, 7c (B 4:28).

[17]"Sed quia ipse actus liberi arbitrii reducitur in Deum sicut in causam, necesse est ut ea quae ex libero arbitrio fiunt divinae providentiae subdantur" 1a. 22, 2, ad 4 (B 5:96).

gaze is eternal and immutable, making all that exists at any time present to him. God is said to know the latter by knowledge of simple understanding, for these things have no existence outside his knowledge.[18] As a further corollary of God's perfect knowledge of all things he creates, Thomas maintains that God also knows evils, for evils are privations to which created things are susceptible.[19]

Thomas has argued, then, that God knows all things in himself. Because he contains all things within himself perfectly, eternally, and immutably, God knows all things at once rather than discursively, and his knowledge is perfect, eternal, and immutable. Given this position, Thomas finds himself confronted with the problem examined in chapter one of reconciling God's knowledge with the contingency of future events. An absolutely omniscient God should, one assumes, know absolutely everything, including contingent future events. If God's knowledge of such events is necessary, infallible, and the cause of the events, however, it would seem that the events themselves must be necessary.

As previously noted, Thomas argues in reply that the divine knowledge contains all worldly events as eternally present and not as future. This doctrine of eternity, again, is best interpreted as timelessness. In that case, the divine knowledge cannot be given a temporal location prior to any event, and the necessity or contingency of an event is dependent solely on the nature of its *proximate* cause.[20]

CHALLENGES TO ETERNAL KNOWLEDGE

Recent years have seen Thomas's doctrine of an eternal divine knowledge criticized in various ways. A number of philosophers

---

[18]"Sed horum quae actu non sunt, est attendenda quaedam diversitas. Quaedam enim, licet non sint nunc in actu, tamen vel fuerunt vel erunt: et omnia ista dicitur Deus scire scientia *visionis*. . . . Quaedam vero sunt in potentia Dei vel creaturae, quae tamen nec sunt nec erunt neque fuerunt. Et respectu horum non dicitur habere scientiam visionis, sed *simplicis intelligentiae*" 1a. 14, 9c (B 4:32).

[19]"Unde, cum sit hoc esse mali, quod est privatio boni, per hoc ipsum quod Deus cognoscit bona, cognoscit etiam mala" 1a. 14, 11c (B 4:36).

[20]1a. 14, 13, ad 1.

have attempted to show that the doctrine of a timelessly omniscient, benevolent, and omnipotent being is not internally consistent. I will first deal with two brief criticisms of Thomas's doctrine and then consider two more fully articulated challenges at greater length.

In his article "Professor Malcolm on God," Robert Coburn argues against the possibility of an eternal, immutable person as follows:

> Surely it is a necessary condition of anything's being a person that it should be capable (logically) of, among other things, doing at least some of the following: remembering, anticipating, reflecting, deliberating, deciding, intending, and acting intentionally. To see that this is so, one need only ask oneself whether anything which necessarily lacked all of the capabilities noted would, under any conceivable circumstances, count as a person. But now an eternal being would necessarily lack all of these capacities inasmuch as their exercise clearly requires that the being exist in time.[21]

Coburn denies a number of mental activities to an eternal (timeless) being—some, like reflecting and deliberating, because they imply temporal duration and others, like remembering, anticipating, and intending, because they imply position in time either before or after their objects. Several of these activities, especially remembering and reflecting, provide us human beings with much of our knowledge. Thus part of Coburn's attack on the personhood of an eternal being would seem to suggest that such a being can have knowledge only in some diminished sense.

While Coburn is correct in claiming that an eternal being cannot anticipate, remember, or reflect, this need not jeopardize the doctrine of a timeless omniscience. In fact, Thomas admits that God cannot anticipate, remember, or reflect; he further shows why these activities are not essential to the divine knowledge.[22] An ability to anticipate or remember is rendered superfluous by the now-familiar claim that all things are present to God. Likewise, the fact that God knows everything at once implies that he has no

---

[21]Robert C. Coburn, "Professor Malcolm on God," *Australasian Journal of Philosophy* 41 (1963): 155.

[22]Pike also makes this point against Coburn; he argues that it is not necessary that knowledge exist in time. See *God and Timelessness*, 123-25.

need to reflect, if reflecting is understood as mental progression from the unknown to the known.[23] Accordingly, all that Coburn's assertions really demonstrate are several ways in which timeless and temporal knowledge are different.[24]

Despite his defense of the doctrine of timeless knowledge as an answer to the problem of divine omniscience and human freedom, Nelson Pike offers a different reason for rejecting the idea of a timeless knower.[25] Pike wonders what evidence we could have for saying that a timeless being knows something. He considers a number of actions whose performance by an individual would give warrant for saying that that individual knew something (e.g., making an assertion, pointing at something, betting on something). Pike maintains that a timeless being could not act in any of these various ways because each implies change and temporal existence. He concludes, therefore, that since we can have no grounds for attributing knowledge to a timeless being, we cannot really understand and hence should reject the idea of a timeless knower.[26]

Defenders of Thomas's doctrine would surely question Pike's appeal for *empirical* evidence to support the claim that God has knowledge. The Thomist would agree that we cannot really or adequately understand timeless knowledge on the model of human temporal knowledge. Nevertheless, he could argue that this does not undermine the concept of timeless knowledge for at least two reasons: First, Pike admits that there is no essential tie between existence in time and the possession of knowledge, and there are no good grounds for holding that the timeless possession of knowledge is logically impossible.[27] Second, appeal to empirical evi-

---

[23] 1a. 14, 7c.

[24] I have here discussed only the cognitive functions of anticipating, remembering, and reflecting. Coburn also mentions deliberating, deciding, and intending, but since these latter are functions of will, they will be considered in chapter three.

[25] Pike, *God and Timelessness*, 125-27.

[26] Ibid., 128.

[27] Ibid., 123-25.

dence that God has knowledge is unnecessary, since God's perfect knowledge is a logical implication of the divine perfection. Such an *a priori* argument is for Thomas sufficient by itself, apart from any empirical evidence, to establish the divine omniscience. Hence neither of these arguments represents a serious challenge to the doctrine of an eternal divine knowledge.

TIMELESS KNOWLEDGE
OF THE PRESENT MOMENT

A somewhat more plausible argument than those discussed above turns on questions of God's knowledge about time itself. Several philosophers have maintained that an immutable being could not know a limited but important set of facts about the passage of time.[28] I will review the most sustained argument for this position, that of Norman Kretzmann in an article entitled "Omniscience and Immutability."[29] Kretzmann argues as follows:

(1) A perfect being is not subject to change. (2) A perfect being knows everything. (3) A being that knows everything always knows what time it is. (4) A being that always knows what time it is is subject to change. ∴(5) A perfect being is subject to change. (6) A perfect being is not a perfect being. ∴(7) There is no perfect being.[30]

Premises (1) and (2), Kretzmann claims, are principles of immutability and omniscience generally ascribed to an absolutely perfect being.[31] Premise (3) is said to be an instance of a logical truth, that is, knowing everything implies knowing what time it is. Assuming "it is now t_n" is the standard form for propositions expressing the time, the state of knowledge of a being that always knows what time it is changes incessantly with respect to propositions of

[28]See A. N. Prior, "The Formalities of Omniscience," 116; Coburn, "Professor Malcolm on God," 155-56; and Tobias Chapman, "Determinism and Omniscience," *Dialogue* 9 (1970): 371.

[29]*Journal of Philosophy* 63 (1966): 409-21.

[30]Kretzmann, "Omniscience and Immutability," 409-10.

[31]Ibid., 409, nn. 1, 2. Kretzmann claims that the principle of immutability is a thesis of orthodox Christian theology and that the principle of omniscience is "even more familiar and less problematic."

the form "it is now t_n." But a being that knows something different from what it used to know has changed; hence premise (4).

In the rest of his article, Kretzmann attempts to defend this argument against a number of objections. Let us first consider Kretzmann's treatment of a serious objection drawn from Aquinas's conception of the divine knowledge.[32] Thomas argues that God has simultaneous rather than successive knowledge of the exact state of the universe at every moment. Given this doctrine of omniscience, Thomas can maintain that God always knows what time it is without being subject to change, since his knowledge includes every event in the universe, the order of events, and which events occur simultaneously with which other events.[33]

Kretzmann does not challenge God's possession of this kind of knowledge. He finds this account of omniscience "drastically incomplete," however, because "an omniscient being must know not only the entire scheme of contingent events from beginning to end at once, but also *at what stage of realization that scheme now is*."[34] But, Kretzmann points out, it is this kind of knowledge that changes continuously and that is referred to in premise (3) of his argument.

What is the force of Kretzmann's reply to this objection? It is important to note that Kretzmann admits a timelessly eternal God can have all knowledge about time that does not require existence at a particular moment; in other words, God can have knowledge *of* time that does not require existence *at* a time. His reply depends on the claim that the use of indexical terms like 'now' indicates the possession of a type of knowledge over and above all "non-temporally-specific" facts about time. What, then, is this special type of information represented by the term 'now'?

---

[32]Kretzmann cites a passage from the *Summa contra Gentiles* 1, 55 as an example of this position. Cf. "Omniscience and Immutability," 413.

[33]This type of knowledge is referred to as 'awareness of time' by Pike, who distinguishes it from 'time of awareness'. Cf. *God and Timelessness*, 11.

[34]Kretzmann, "Omniscience and Immutability," 414 (italics in original).

Kretzmann describes it as the "stage of realization" of the scheme of contingent events, or simply, "what is going on."[35]

Thomas can, however, insist that God knows "the stage of realization achieved" or "what is going on" for *every* 'now' if he knows the whole scheme of events at once. It has been argued that the term 'now' merely expresses the simultaneity of the production (utterance or writing) of that term with something else—as in the statement "it is now two o'clock," for example, with a particular time designation like 2:00 p.m. CST, December 3, 1978.[36] If this is the case, then God could clearly have (timeless) knowledge of all the correlations between events in time to which terms like 'now' refer.[37]

To this statement of the objection, Kretzmann may reply that *he* means something more by the term 'now', namely the direct and "vivid" experience of certain events as *present*, which differentiates them from all past and future events. This, Kretzmann might contend, is lacking in God since it depends on experience *in* time, the continuous movement or passage of events from the future through the present into the past. Kretzmann's case, in other words, seems to depend on the uniqueness and the importance of temporal passage and of the immediacy of the present.

Kretzmann apparently feels that the cognitive significance of experience in time is self-evident, since he offers no argument to support it. There are, however, at least two strong arguments *against* ascribing cognitive significance to this kind of experience.

---

[35]Ibid., 414, 417.

[36]J. J. C. Smart points out that this is the analysis of 'now' offered by Goodman, Reichenbach, and Quine. Similar analyses are provided for the terms 'past', 'present', and 'future' and for verb tenses. See *Problems of Space and Time*, ed. J. J. C. Smart (New York: Macmillan, 1964) 18.

[37]Both Castañeda and Pike arrive at this conclusion. They argue that although statements containing indexicals are personal, intransferable, and ephemeral, their meaning can be captured in statements free of indexicals. These latter statements can be known by a timeless and immutable God. See Hector-Neri Castañeda, "Omniscience and Indexical Reference," *Journal of Philosophy* 64 (1967): 203-10; *God and Timelessness*, 91-95.

First, a number of philosophers of science have argued that human experience of time as moving or of events as becoming is merely a subjective psychological phenomenon, which has no correlate in the physical world.[38] This conclusion is based on the relativistic conception of the world as a four-dimensional space-time continuum in which the time dimension is as fixed and immovable as the dimensions of space.[39] If this conception is correct, then the movement of time and the special status of events experienced as present are nothing more than illusions. Kretzmann makes no mention of this conception, but he does consider an objection to his argument that bears some similarity to it.

According to this objection, a perfect being transcends time and is therefore not subject to change, since change occurs only in time.[40] Kretzmann considers an interpretation of this objection to the effect that "from a God's eye point of view there is no time, that time is a universal human illusion."[41] He admits that this interpretation is able to overturn his argument, but claims that the cost of denying the reality of time is too high. This objection is based on the unreality of time. In fact, neither the divine knowledge nor the four-dimensional conception of the universe need deny the reality of time itself, rather only the reality of temporal *passage*. Perhaps we do pay a high price for giving up the reality of temporal passage, but Kretzmann offers no reason why this is so.

Second, even if human experience of temporal passage is not a mere illusion, it may still be considered a limitation, since it implies that one cannot know the whole time sequence with the same immediacy and clarity that is ascribed to each present moment. In other words, even if there is some objective correlate to

---

[38]Cf. Adolf Grünbaum, "Time, Irreversible Processes, and the Physical Status of Becoming," in *Problems of Space and Time*, 397-425, and Donald C. Williams, "The Myth of Passage," *Journal of Philosophy* 48 (1951): 457-72.

[39]Cf. Moritz Schlick, "The Four-Dimensional World," and H. Minkowski, "Space and Time," both in *Problems of Space and Time*, 292-312.

[40]Kretzmann, "Omniscience and Immutability," 415.

[41]Ibid.

the experience of temporal passage or "presentiality," this kind of experience would rule out a more comprehensive grasp of events in time. This kind of experience should therefore be viewed as a defective mode of knowledge and not be deemed necessary for the divine knowledge.

Kretzmann considers an objection along these lines, namely, that a perfect being's omniscience cannot include strictly everything, but rather "everything the knowing of which does not impair its perfection."[42] Kretzmann denies this objection as an arbitrary limitation of God's knowledge, but in fact, some limitation of omniscience does appear to be necessary. For instance, God's knowledge cannot include the actual experience of physical pain or despair (since being in these states would imply imperfection), though God can, of course, know *about* physical pain and despair in every way that does not require the actual experience of these or some other defects. Kretzmann does not consider these cases, but he does make the following (unsupported) claims regarding conflicts between two kinds of knowledge:

> There is no reason to suspect that there *are* things that would if known limit the knower's capacity for knowledge. More directly to the point at issue in the argument, there is no reason whatever to think that knowing what is going on is a kind of knowing that limits the knower's capacity for knowledge.[43]

If experience in time includes some information that a timeless knowledge cannot include, it seems clear that timeless knowledge also includes much information that experience in time cannot include, in particular a synoptic vision of all temporal events at once. If this is the case, then experience in time would clearly limit one's capacity for a more comprehensive knowledge. Experience in time would then be denied to God for just the same reason as experience in a physical body is denied to God—because it would conflict with the divine perfection.

In summary, then, I have tried to show that Kretzmann's argument derives its plausibility from the importance we attach to

---

[42]Ibid., 417.

[43]Ibid., 418.

experience in time. Although there may be some reason to think that a being lacking experience in time is deficient in certain ways, Kretzmann does not make a case for the *cognitive* imperfection of such a timeless being. Moreover, Thomas may claim that the ability to have experience in time, like the ability to feel pain, is a deficient mode of knowing and hence cannot be ascribed to God.

TIMELESS KNOWLEDGE AND PERFECTION

In the preceding section, the doctrine of a timeless omniscience was defended against an attack by Kretzmann on its internal consistency. A more serious challenge to this doctrine focuses not on its internal coherence, but on its adequacy in accounting for an important relationship between God and the world. This challenge is ultimately directed against Thomas's doctrines of divine perfection and love; it calls into question the claim that a purely actual and immutable state of being constitutes the fullness of perfection. We will consider this challenge as stated first by a philosopher clearly sympathetic to the Thomistic system and then by an outspoken critic of St. Thomas.

In his article "A New Look at the Immutability of God," Father W. Norris Clarke suggests a revision of the principles of divine timelessness and immutability.[44] Clarke expresses sympathy with modern critics of the Thomistic doctrine of the immutability of God, especially those who claim that a genuine personal relationship with God is impossible unless God is able to respond to man's contingent actions. Clarke proposes, therefore, to modify the Thomistic doctrine of unconditional immutability while still remaining within a Thomistic metaphysical framework. He hopes in this way to show how a loving interpersonal dialogue between God and his creatures is possible. Clarke emphasizes that his proposal must be compatible with the fundamental notion of God's

---

[44]W. Norris Clarke, S. J., "A New Look at the Immutability of God," in *God Knowable and Unknowable*, ed. Robert J. Roth (New York: Fordham University Press, 1973) 43-72.

absolute or infinite perfection, since this notion should remain constant and shape all the rest of the divine attributes.[45]

Clarke's proposed modification of the doctrine of divine immutability is based on his development of a distinction made in Thomistic metaphysics between the orders of real and intentional being.[46] What the doctrine of immutability must rule out, according to Clarke, is the possibility of change in God's "intrinsic real being," since any such change implies an increase (or decrease) in the ontological perfection of the being undergoing change and is therefore incompatible with infinite perfection. Clarke allows, however, that change can occur in the "intentional content" of the divine consciousness as God knows and wills new creatures. This, he claims, is not a change in God's intrinsic real being.[47]

Clarke's account already contains a significant departure from Thomas's doctrine, since Thomas makes no distinction between real and intentional being in God. Rather, Thomas claims that in God both knowledge *and* the object of knowledge are identical to the divine essence.[48] Even if we disregard this passage and grant Clarke a distinction between the real intrinsic being of God and the objects of divine consciousness,[49] Clarke must also show that these two are not related in such a way that change in the latter implies change in the former. Clarke's suggestion that these two are, in fact, independent of one another seems plausible only because he fails to make a further distinction between change in

---

[45]Ibid., 46-47.

[46]Clarke states this distinction as follows: "St. Thomas distinguishes between (1) the being or existence of a thing in its own right, with its own intrinsic act of existence or 'natural being', by which the thing exists with its own nature in itself and not merely as an object of thought in a mind (its *esse naturale, esse in re,* or *in rerum natura*) and (2) the mode of being which it has as an object of knowledge (or love) existing or present in the consciousness of a knower (or lover), which he calls its 'intentional being' . . . (*esse intentionale, esse cognitum, esse volitum*)" Ibid., 53.

[47]Ibid., 49.

[48]See p. 32 above.

[49]This distinction does seem important for Thomas later, given his postulation of a multiplicity of ideas in the mind of God. See 1a. 15, 2.

the *objects of consciousness* and change in the *consciousness of objects*. Clarke ascribes change to the "field of intentional consciousness" in God,[50] yet such a change does not affect only the order of intentional being; it also implies that the divine consciousness itself changes in taking account of new objects.[51] But the divine consciousness is clearly not in the order of intentional being. It does not exist only "as an object of knowledge," but is also God's "own intrinsic act of existence," his intrinsic real being. According to Thomas's doctrine, it is not possible to permit change in the divine consciousness but deny change in God's "intrinsic real being."

Clarke's position seems to depend not on the distinction between real and intentional being, but rather on a distinction between the determinate states and the general nature of the divine consciousness. This distinction would allow Clarke to make his point that although the states of divine consciousness may change, its perfect nature remains constant. Therefore, change in the focus of divine consciousness would in no way compromise the divine perfection, which must be affirmed of God above all. In support of this claim, Clarke argues that God's knowledge of a finite being, though it is an additional item of knowledge, must not be thought of as a higher fullness of knowing, but rather as an inner determination or limitation of God's infinitely perfect knowledge of himself. God's knowledge of our free actions is thus determined by us, but only in the sense that we channel or delimit (and partially negate) the flow of God's indeterminate plenitude of power so as to accomplish our own ends.[52]

Based on his acceptance of change and succession in the divine consciousness, Clarke also prefers a durational model of the divine eternity to the durationless model, which he claims is clearly the view of Boethius and Thomas.[53] While Thomas claims

---

[50]Clarke, "A New Look," 50.

[51]In fact, the intentional objects may not change at all except in coming into and going out of consciousness.

[52]Clarke, "A New Look," 68.

[53]Ibid., 60, 64.

that God sees the whole of history in a single, simultaneous vision (*tota simul*), Clarke conceives the contents of the divine consciousness as constantly and endlessly expanding to include the ongoing evolution of temporal history.[54] Clarke also claims that although God does not know the as yet undetermined aspects of the future, this does not constitute an imperfection in his knowledge, since those aspects are not in themselves knowable.

We have seen that Clarke's departure from Thomas's doctrine of divine knowledge is more significant than he seems willing to admit. Clarke also claims that his account does not deviate from the fundamental Thomistic principle of God's absolute perfection, but in fact, his solution of the problem of immutability is not compatible with Thomas's notion of perfection. Thomas accepts the priority of the actual and determinate over the potential and general, based on the principle of sufficient reason, and hence his notion of perfection includes complete actuality and the absence of potentiality.[55]

For Thomas, then, absolute perfection would consist in the actual existence of all possible value, and absolutely perfect knowledge would consist in completely necessary and determinate rather than merely general and contingent knowledge.[56] Thomas consequently would reject Clarke's account of change in the divine consciousness as well as his reference to an indeterminate plenitude of divine power on the grounds that each implies a lack of complete actuality and hence is incompatible with absolute perfection. Knowledge that changes implies potentiality and contingency, but in Thomas's view these are defects and therefore cannot be imputed to God. Despite Clarke's desire to remain close to Thomas, the "new look at the immutability of God" he presents requires basic changes in Thomas's doctrines of divine knowledge and divine perfection.

In a commentary on Aquinas's doctrine of the divine nature, Charles Hartshorne also criticizes Thomas's claim that knowl-

---

[54]Ibid., 65.

[55]1a. 4, 2.

[56]1a. 14, 11; 1a. 14, 13.

edge does not cause a real change in God.[57] Hartshorne has serious doubts about the value of immutable knowledge in God. He maintains that Thomas's understanding of divine knowledge makes God more like the inanimate object of an act of knowing than the active human knower who is changed in coming to know something new.

He refers to Thomas's example of the relation between a man and a pillar to illustrate what he finds problematic in Thomas's account of the divine knowledge. Thomas uses this example to demonstrate that God's relation to the world is a "relation of reason" (*relatio rationis*), dependent on human reason and not on any change or dependence in God himself.[58] Thomas claims in this example that the relation "being on the right of" is really in the man (presumably because the man consciously assumes that position in relation to the pillar), but not really in the pillar (presumably because the pillar itself is not affected by the man's position). Analogously, Thomas claims that all creatures are ordered to God, but in God there is no real relation to creatures. Hartshorne contends that this whole passage makes God seem more like an inanimate object of knowledge (the pillar) than an active subject of knowledge (the man). He concludes that Thomas's God lacks an important kind of awareness, making him more like a "superobject" than a "supersubject."

Though the tone of Hartshorne's remarks is much more critical than that of Clarke's, both take issue with the doctrine of a timelessly complete knowledge because it excludes responsiveness and development. The absence of these two attributes is thought to constitute a genuine weakness or imperfection in the divine knowledge, because it interferes with a reciprocal personal relationship between God and man (Clarke) and with the idea of an active, personal divine life (Hartshorne). Thus both Clarke and Hartshorne are concerned about the relationship between eternal divine knowledge and divine action. The next chapter will be de-

---

[57]*Philosophers Speak of God*, ed. Charles Hartshorne and William Reese (Chicago: University of Chicago Press, 1953) 131-33.

[58]1a. 13, 7.

voted to a fuller examination of the relationship between divine timelessness and action.

Finally, since Clarke and Hartshorne reject Thomas's notion of perfection, it may be asked what principle of divine perfection, if any, they would prefer. Hartshorne does propose an alternative principle of perfection, which will be examined in chapter four.

KNOWLEDGE AND ANALOGY

A standard Thomistic reply to arguments like those of Kretzmann, Clarke, and Hartshorne holds that they do not take into consideration the fact that the term 'knowledge' is predicated of God and man *analogously*, and hence they adduce false consequences regarding divine knowledge from facts about human knowledge. This reply is based on Thomas's doctrine of analogy, a type of predication that Thomas uses to explain human knowledge of God, among other things. Thomas holds that analogous terms fall somewhere between equivocal and univocal terms. A term is said to be equivocal when it has completely different meanings in different instances (e.g., 'dog' for the animal and the star). A term is said to be univocal if it has the same meaning in different instances (e.g., 'man' for Plato and Socrates). An analogous term, then, is one whose meaning is partly shared and partly different in different instances. How and to what extent the meaning of an analogous term is shared and how it differs, though, is a matter of long-standing dispute among interpreters of Thomas.

For one thing, there seems to have been some change in Thomas's own thinking about analogy: in *de Veritate* he holds that proper proportionality is the only valid type of analogy between God and creatures, but this type of analogy is not used at all in the later writings.[59] Apart from *de Veritate*, Thomas describes the relationship between God and creatures in terms of many different analogies, including reference, proportion, imitation, priority, participation, and eminence.[60] These kinds of analogy are usually

---

[59]George P. Klubertanz, S. J., *St. Thomas Aquinas on Analogy* (Chicago: Loyola University Press, 1960) 109.

[60]Ibid., 106.

grounded in the causal relationship of God and creatures; that is, the doctrine that as their cause, God must possess all the perfections of creatures in some higher manner. The same perfections, then, are possessed eminently by God and participated in by creatures. In human knowledge, however, perfections are first *recognized* in creatures and then attributed to God, but without the limitations inherent in finite created existence.

The outline of Thomas's doctrine of divine knowledge provided earlier in this chapter clearly depends on an analogous relationship between human and divine knowledge. Where human knowledge is incomplete, discursive, and dependent on external objects, divine knowledge is held to be complete, intuitive, and self-sufficient. But if this is what is meant by the claim that human and divine knowledge are related analogously, it is not clear how the doctrine of analogy can be used to respond to Clarke and Hartshorne. The criticisms of these philosophers take account of the above-mentioned differences between divine and human knowledge. In fact, it is precisely the idea of an immutable divine knowledge of all things that they challenge.

There is, however, no special reason for holding that only those differences noted above separate the divine and human senses of 'knowledge'. They may be only the most prominent differences. In fact, for every attempt to infer from human conceptions of knowledge a conclusion about divine knowledge that conflicts with Thomas's doctrine, one may reply on Thomas's behalf that the aspect in question is one in which human and divine knowledge differ. Each time this defense is invoked, however, it further restricts the content of Thomas's doctrine of divine knowledge.

Thomas appears, at least, to be speaking quite literally about some aspects of God's knowledge. For instance, the terms 'immutable' and 'all things' in "immutable knowledge of all things" do not seem to mean something entirely different when predicated of divine knowledge than when predicated of anything else. In the case of immutability, it is clear that divine immutability must be understood somewhat differently from the immutability of a rock, or even of a star; but if anything, God's immutability is held to be more complete and radical than that of any creature.[61] As for the term 'all things', Thomas quite explicitly includes under this term both universals and particulars, including contingent events.[62] Thus the "things" in question would seem to be the same for God and man, though God may be said to know each thing more fully. The criticisms of Clarke and Hartshorne, however, seem to derive much of their force from just this basic understanding of the concept of an immutable knowledge of all things.

The doctrine of analogy may then be used on Thomas's behalf to deny the relevance of any particular criticism of his doctrine based on human experience. As long as a univocal core of meaning can be established for basic terms like 'immutable' and 'all things', however, Clarke and Hartshorne are able to press their criticisms of Thomas's doctrine of the divine knowledge.

In a later passage of the *Summa Theologiae* on the subject of grace, Thomas calls into question the efficacy of natural reason in achieving any knowledge about "more profound intelligible realities" including, perhaps, the divine nature.[63] Such knowledge, Thomas claims, can only be achieved through the light of grace in faith or prophecy. This approach bears a strong resemblance to the logic of obedience discussed in the introduction. It emphasizes the importance of grace rather than natural reason for knowledge of God and suggests that metaphysics be abandoned in favor of the revealed truths of Scripture. An interpretation of Thomas based on this concept of grace would remain untouched by philosophical objections like those of Clarke and Hartshorne, since those objections presuppose that Thomas's concern (at least in his treatise on the divine nature)[64] is with natural theology: the statement of a

---

[61]1a. 9, 2.

[62]See p. 33 above.

[63]"Sic igitur intellectus humanus habet aliquam formam, scilicet ipsum intelligibile lumen quod est de se sufficiens ad quaedam intelligibilia cognoscenda, ad ea scilicet in quorum notitiam per sensibilia possumus devenire. Altiora vero intelligibilia intellectus humanus cognoscere non potest, nisi fortiori lumine perficiatur, sicut lumine fidei vel prophetiae, quod dicitur lumen gratiae, inquantum est naturae superadditum" 1a2ae. 109, 1c (B 30:70).

[64]1a. 2-1a. 26.

doctrine of God based on natural reason apart from articles of faith or revelation. This would seem to be the most natural interpretation of the first part of the *Summa*, since it clearly emphasizes rational argument over appeals to Scripture.[65] If the claim that Thomas views grace and not reason as the vehicle for knowledge of God can be sustained, the purpose and value of Thomas's doctrine of God in the Prima Pars no longer seems clear. Interpreted as natural theology, it would seem to be doomed to failure.

---

[65] At 1a. 12, 12, Thomas acknowledges that we can have some, although not complete, knowledge of God through natural reason.

CHAPTER THREE

THE DOCTRINE OF ETERNAL WILL AND ACTION

The previous chapter was devoted to an examination of Thomas's doctrine of divine eternity (or timelessness) as it bears on God's knowledge. In this chapter I will continue to explore the doctrine of timelessness, this time in its relationship to the divine will and act of creation. As in chapter two, I will first review Thomas's accounts of will and creation, then attempt to evaluate them.

AQUINAS ON DIVINE WILL AND CREATION

The existence of will in God, Thomas maintains, follows from the existence of the divine mind, since any being that apprehends the good mentally also seeks to gain it and rests with it when it is gained, and these latter two activities are functions of will.[1] As

---

[1]"Unde et natura intellectualis ad bonum apprehensum per formam intelligibilem similem habitudinem habet; ut scilicet cum habet ipsum quiescat in illo, cum vero non habet quaerat ipsum; et utrumque pertinet ad voluntatem" 1a. 19, 1c (B 5:4).

Thomas explains in the reply to an objection, God already possesses his own self-sufficient goodness, and therefore he does not have will in the sense of unfulfilled desire, but only in the sense of delighting in his own goodness.[2] Using an analogy with reproduction in animals, however, Thomas expands the notion of divine will to include God's "communicating" or sharing his goodness by creating other things.[3] Thomas cautions that this does not imply that God is moved by anything outside himself, though, since God wills creatures only as a manifestation of his own goodness. God wills his own goodness necessarily, but since his goodness is completely self-sufficient and independent of other things, he is not constrained to will any creatures at all, much less any particular creature.[4]

Hence though he wills that other things partake of his goodness, God's willing his goodness is not the cause of his willing other things. God's willing of creatures, therefore, is completely free.[5] According to Thomas, then, the activity of will in God is twofold: (1) it rests in or delights in the divine goodness, and (2) it shares that goodness by willing the existence of other things. Once a thing is willed, it cannot be unwilled, since the divine will, like the divine knowledge, is immutable.[6]

---

[2]"Voluntas in nobis pertinet ad appetitivam partem; quae, licet ab appetendo nominetur, non tamen hunc solum habet actum ut appetat quae non habet, sed etiam ut amet quod habet et delectetur in illo. Et quantum ad hoc voluntas in Deo ponitur, quae semper habet bonum quod est ejus objectum" 1a. 19, 1c (B 5:6).

[3]"Unde si res naturales inquantum perfectae sunt suum bonum aliis communicant, multo magis pertinet ad voluntatem divinam ut bonum suum aliis per similitudem communicet, secundum quod possibile est" 1a. 19, 2c (B 5:14).

[4]"Unde cum bonitas Dei sit perfecta et esse possit sine aliis, cum nihil ei perfectionis ex aliis accrescat, sequitur quod alia a se eum velle non sit necessarium absolute" 1a. 19, 3c (B 5:14).

[5]Cf. 1a. 19, 10.

[6]"Et tamen necessarium est ex suppositione. Supposito enim quod velit, non potest non velle, quia non potest voluntas ejus mutari" 1a. 19, 3c (B 5:14). Cf. also 1a. 19, 7.

Thomas then reaffirms his earlier statement that the combined activity of knowledge and will in God is the cause of all things; in so doing, he rejects the hypothesis of a necessary emanation of things from the divine nature. Moreover, God's will is inevitably fulfilled, since no particular cause can interfere with the action of the universal cause. Nevertheless, Thomas claims that although God does not will moral evil, he does permit it to occur.[7]

God carries out his will regarding creatures in his act of creation. Thomas defines creation as "the issuing forth of all being from God";[8] he admits that this involves a sequence from nonbeing to being, but denies that it can strictly be called a change. Change for Thomas requires the existence of an underlying subject of change that remains constant, either an individual substance in accidental change or a quantity of matter in substantial change. No such subject exists in creation, since God uses no prior material to bring things into existence. Thomas understands creation, therefore, not as a change, but as a relation of the creature to the creator as the origin of its existence.[9]

This relation is said to be real in the creature alone; it is also attributed to God because of the creature's dependence on him,

---

[7]"Deus igitur neque vult mala fieri, neque vult mala non fieri, sed vult permittere mala fieri" 1a. 19, 9 ad 3 (B 5:42).

[8]"Oportet considerare ... emanationem totius entis a causa universali, quae est Deus; et hanc quidem emanationem designamus nomine creationis" 1a. 45, 1c (B 8:26).

[9]"Nam de ratione mutationis est quod aliquid idem se habeat aliter nunc et prius: nam quandoque est idem ens actu, aliter se habens nunc et prius, sicut in motibus secundum quantitatem et qualitatem et ubi; quandoque vero est idem ens in potentia tantum, sicut in mutatione secundum substantiam, cujus subjectum est materia. Sed in creatione, per quam producitur tota substantia rerum, non potest accipi aliquid idem aliter se habens nunc et prius, nisi secundum intellectum tantum, sicut si intelligatur aliqua res prius non fuisse totaliter, et postea esse. Sed cum actio et passio conveniant in substantia motus et differant solum secundum habitudines diversas, ut dicitur in *Physic.* [202a20], oportet quod subtracto motu non remaneant nisi diversae habitudines in creante et creato" 1a. 45, 2 ad 2 (B 8:32).

but not because of any change in God himself.[10] It is claimed that
the divine act of creation does not occur at a particular time, since
it produces both creatures and time itself. A time is assigned to
the beginning of the world, however, in order to show that the
world did not always exist.[11] Thomas also contends that one could
think of God as existing before the world in an everlasting imaginary time[12]—imaginary because it contains no changing
beings, and time is just the measurement of change.

The above accounts of divine will and creation suggest a possible tension in Thomas's doctrine. On the one hand, Thomas contends that the divine life, the supreme mode of being, is
immutable and eternal. This eternity, as argued earlier, is best interpreted as timelessness. Therefore, it would seem that the divine will and creation must also be eternal (timeless) properties.
On the other hand, Thomas recognizes that as objects of the divine
will and products of creation, we and all other creatures share a
different, *temporal* mode of existence. Due to this basic difference
of divine will and action from the world of creatures, the relation
between them is very difficult to characterize. How, that is, can we

---

[10]"Creatio active significata significat actionem divinam, quae est ejus essentia cum relatione ad creaturam. Sed relatio in Deo ad creaturam non est realis, sed secundum rationem tantum. Relatio vero creaturae ad Deum est relatio
realis, ut supra dictum est, cum de divinis nominibus ageretur [1a. 13, 7]" 1a.
45, 3 ad 1 (B 8:36). At 1a. 13, 7c (B 3:74), this relation is explained as follows:
"Cum igitur Deus sit extra totum ordinem creaturae, et omnes creaturae ordi-
nentur ad ipsum, et non e converso, manifestum est quod creaturae realiter referuntur ad ipsum Deum; sed in Deo non est aliqua realis relatio ejus ad
creaturas, sed secundum rationam tantum, in quantum creaturae referuntur ad
ipsum."

[11]"Sed in agente universali, quod producit rem et tempus, non est considerare quod agat nunc et non prius secundum imaginationem temporis post tempus, quasi tempus praesupponatur ejus actioni; sed considerandum est, quod
dedit effectui suo tempus quantum voluit, et secundum quod conveniens fuit ad
suam potentiam demonstrandam. Manifestius enim mundus ducit in cogniti-
onem divinae potentiae creantis si mundus non semper fuit quam si semper fuis-
set" 1a. 46, 1 ad 6 (B 8:74).

[12]"Deus est prior mundo duratione. Sed *ly* 'prius' non designat prioritatem
temporis, sed aeternitatis. Vel dicendum quod designat aeternitatem temporis
imaginati et non realiter existentis" 1a. 46, 1 ad 8 (B 8:74).

understand the relation of a will and action not bound by the limits of time to objects that do exist in time?

One reply to this question is simply that we *cannot* understand God's relation to man, that even the fundamental nature of the divine will and action is beyond human comprehension. But such a reply would be premature, as Thomas does suggest two ways to understand this relation. Sometimes he claims that the relation is a nominal, not a real one in the divine case; that is, it does not refer to anything in the divine essence.[13] In other passages Thomas seems to be willing to ascribe some sense of temporality to God in order to explain his relationship to the world.[14] It is worthwhile to first consider the nature of the conceptual problem involved here and then examine each of Thomas's explanations in turn.

WILL, ACTION, AND CAUSATION

Much, if not most, of the recent philosophical activity called "action theory" consists in attempts to articulate the special features of certain kinds of events, which allow them to count as the *actions* of particular individuals. Wittgenstein provided a now-famous impetus for this enterprise.

> Let us not forget this: When I raise my arm, my arm goes up. And the problem arises: what is left over if I subtract the fact that my arm goes up from the fact that I raise my arm?[15]

Under what conditions, in other words, can we conclude that the occurrence of an event (my arm going up) was the result of an action I perform (raising my arm)?

Several recent analyses of action attempt to answer this question by arguing that the events at issue are related in particular ways to the wants, intentions, and beliefs of an individual. Thus

---

[13]See n. 10 above.

[14]See n. 11 above.

[15]Ludwig Wittgenstein, *Philosophical Investigations* (Oxford: Blackwell, 1953) par. 621.

Arthur Danto concludes that the relation between actions and intentions or reasons is one of causation.

> . . . there is no trying unless there is an intention: and this is a conceptual truth. But no other condition really is required in order that intentions, to be sure against the background of internalized argument, should be causes. Their satisfaction of the status of causes is entailed by the concept of mediated action. If there are mediated actions, there are basic actions, and these are caused by intentions or, speaking more loosely, by reasons.[16]

Similarly, Alvin Goldman holds that a set of wants and beliefs, called an "action plan," causes intentional actions.[17] In a slightly different vein, Hugh McCann argues that a particular kind of mental action, called a "volition," is the basic cause of its object by initiating the appropriate physical action.[18]

This brief excursus into the analysis of action may help to illustrate the difficulty involved in explicating a doctrine of timeless will and action in God. A question similar to that posed by Wittgenstein may be asked about the divine act of creation: What is left over if we subtract the fact that the world exists from the fact that God created the world? Or, to be more specific, under what conditions can we conclude that the occurrence of a particular "event" (namely, the existence of the world) was the result of an action performed by God (namely, his creation)? The analyses of action mentioned above would suggest that an answer to these questions must include the claim that some feature of the divine mind (intentions, wants and beliefs, or volitions) *causes* the existence of the world.

This general claim is, of course, reminiscent of an assertion of Thomas we have already noted, namely that the divine will, together with divine knowledge, is the cause of all things. Mc-

---

[16]Arthur Danto, *Analytical Philosophy of Action* (Cambridge: Cambridge University Press, 1973) 194.

[17]Alvin I. Goldman, *A Theory of Human Action* (Englewood Cliffs NJ: Prentice-Hall, 1970) 57.

[18]Hugh McCann, "Volition and Basic Action," *Philosophical Review* 83 (1974): 466-72.

Cann's defense of volitions as causally basic mental actions seems especially appropriate here. Thomas's view of God's act of willing the world would appear to agree with McCann's analysis of volition in two respects: (1) volition is a distinct, intentional mental action, not just a mental state, and (2) volition has causal efficacy. God, of course, is held to create the world solely by means of volitional acts. Yet Thomas also maintains that God chooses to achieve certain of his intentions by means of physical instruments like human beings.[19] These mediated divine actions would, then, correspond in humans to bodily movements initiated by volitional actions.

If the general view of human action cited above is correct, then the will-action-result relationship is a special case of the cause-effect relationship. Both of these relationships, however, appear to have unavoidable temporal implications, at least in those instances where one of the relata is itself a temporal entity. Causes may either be simultaneous with or precede their effects, and actions exemplify both of these relationships. For example, the action of raising my arm and its result, my arm going up, are simultaneous; but the action of my killing Smith (by shooting him, let's say) precedes its result, Smith's death.

It appears to be a conceptual truth, however, that causes cannot temporally succeed their effects. Part of our intuitive notion of a cause is "that which produces or brings about its effect." Obviously, this "action" of producing or bringing about an effect cannot occur if the cause does not exist. Therefore, the effect cannot exist *before* its cause. Danto offers a formal analysis of causal dependency whereby the instantiation of one event type is a necessary condition for the instantiation of another event type.[20] If this is the case, the latter event type (the effect) cannot exist without the former (the cause). But if we suppose that an effect precedes its cause, then there is a time when the effect exists without its cause. On this analysis of causation, therefore, we must also conclude that an effect cannot precede its cause.

---

[19]1a. 103, 6c.

[20]Danto, *Analytical Philosophy of Action*, 93-94.

Similar problems arise in attempting to explicate the relationship between a timeless cause and a temporal effect. Rather than the absurd claim that an effect is the product of a cause that does not yet exist, we are now faced with the mysterious claim that an effect occurring at a particular time is the product of an entity that does not exist at that time nor at any earlier or later time, but instead exists in a timeless, changeless mode. Given this fundamental difference between the modes of existence of God and the world, there appears to be no common ground on which we can establish a causal relationship between them. Indeed, the problem before us now is the reverse of the one we confronted in chapter one. There, the doctrine of timelessness was invoked in order to deny the existence of a determining relationship between divine knowledge and human action. Given the doctrine of divine timelessness, however, we appear to lack the basis for understanding a causal relationship between God and the world.

Obviously, I have not argued for the *impossibility* of a causal relationship between timeless and temporal beings.[21] I have instead suggested that such a relationship must be very different from our ordinary understanding of causality, and hence it must remain largely mysterious to us. Nevertheless, we might appeal to the divine omnipotence to argue that God *can* timelessly cause the world to exist in time. Moreover, we might appeal to some version of the cosmological or teleological arguments to claim that God *must* cause the world. If we also accept Thomas's assertion that God acts causally through his timeless knowledge and will, how might we imagine these to produce the actual temporal sequence of events in the world? Following McCann's suggestion, we might postulate a set of timeless volitional actions whose contents include every event in time ("Let $x_1, y_1, z_1, \ldots$ occur at time t_1,"

---

[21]Nelson Pike, for one, defends this stronger claim. He compares the verb 'creates' to 'produces' and other more specialized "production verbs." He argues that temporal relations are part of the essence of these verbs, and hence God cannot timelessly bring about a temporal state of affairs. See *God and Timelessness*, 101-107.

"Let x_2, y_2, z_2, . . . occur at t_2, . . .").[22] Each event, then, would be timelessly willed to occur at the time specified for it. The set of these volitions, timelessly and unchangeably copresent in the divine mind, would constitute divine providence.

Even this minimal account of divine causal action has serious drawbacks, however. First, in this account, the temporal process of the world is viewed as the unfolding of a timelessly complete set of divine volitions. Despite the assumption of timelessness, it offers a world determined in all of its details by the divine will. Thus divine causality, *even if it is timeless*, results in a conflict between divine *will* and human freedom similar to the conflict between divine *knowledge* and human freedom discussed in chapter one.

A second problem involves the notion of a timeless volition itself. As McCann points out, an essential feature of the notion of volition as action is that it be intentional, or under the control of the agent.[23] In human action this question of intentionality appears to depend not on what is brought about *by* an action, but rather how the action *itself* is brought about. An intentional action must arise out of (or, Danto and Goldman would argue, must be caused by) the beliefs, wants, and intentions of the agent. But our notions of production and causality, strained in the attempt to relate God and the world, are even less appropriate for explaining timeless relations *within* the divine mind. Whether, therefore, the concept of intentional action can be ascribed to timeless divine volitions would seem to have no clear answer.

If, as the above discussion suggests, time plays an essential role in the logic of action and causation, these human concepts obviously cannot provide an adequate model for the notions of timeless will and action. Thomas appears to have some desire to overcome this limitation, since he makes at least two attempts to

---

[22]This account of divine volition bears some resemblance to R. M. Martin's attempt to base a doctrine of God on the notion of "primordial obligations," defined as timeless desires or wishes regarding creatures and worldly events. See "On God and Primordiality," *Review of Metaphysics* 29 (1976): 497-522.

[23]McCann, "Volition and Basic Action," 472.

give a different account of the relationship between God and the world. These two attempts will be examined in turn.

DIVINE ACTION AS
RELATIO RATIONIS TANTUM

In several passages Thomas contrasts the "real relation" (*relatio realis*) creatures bear to God with the "relation merely of reason" (*relatio rationis tantum*) God bears to creatures.[24] The relation of creatures to God is said to be real on the grounds that creatures are wholly dependent on their creator. By calling the relation of God to creatures a relation merely of reason, however, Thomas means that the linking of God to creatures *in time* occurs only in the human mind, since change may not be ascribed to God.[25] Thomas often uses the relations *being knowable by* and *knowing* as examples of this kind of relation.[26] Knowing something is said to be a reality in the mind or senses of the knower, since it makes a real difference to these, but being knowable is not a reality in the thing known, since the thing known is not changed merely by being known.

In this way Thomas can avoid the consequence that there is something temporal in God, namely, a temporal relation to creatures. This strategy "solves" the problem of explaining a temporal relationship of God to creatures by denying that any such relationship exists—except in the human mind.[27] It creates another problem, though, for it would require denying that God really

---

[24]1a. 13, 7; 1a. 28, 1; 1a. 45, 1 ad 3; *de Ver.* 1, 5 ad 16; *de Ver.* 4, 5c.

[25]"Aliquanda vero respectus significatus per ea quae dicuntur ad aliquid est tantum in ipsa apprehensione rationis conferentis unum alteri; et tunc est relatio rationis tantum, sicut cum comparat ratio hominem animali ut speciem ad genus" 1a. 28, 1c (B 6:24). Also "sed in Deo non est aliqua realis relatio ejus ad creaturas, sed secundum rationam tantum, in quantum creaturae referuntur ad ipsum. Et sic nihil prohibet hujusmodi nomina importantia relationam ad creaturam praedicari de Deo ex tempore, non propter aliquam mutationem ipsius, sed propter creaturae mutationem" 1a. 13, 7c (B 3:74).

[26]Cf., e.g., 1a. 13, 7c; *de Ver.* 1, 5 ad 16; *de Ver.* 4, 5c.

[27]The relations of willing and knowing creatures may still be attributed to God if it is held that these are eternal relations.

bears relationships like creator and savior to creatures, since these relationships seem to have temporal implications.[28]

Thomas appears to be faced with a trilemma regarding relations like the divine creation and salvation of creatures. He can affirm one of the following: (1) Such relationships are not really in God, but *secundum rationem tantum*, since creatures are really dependent on him. This solution preserves the divine immutability, but it makes Thomas's doctrine of God uncomfortably similar to Aristotle's in the sense that God appears to be unconcerned with worldly events. (2) Such relationships are really in God, and they do have temporal implications. This solution, however, conflicts with divine immutability. (3) Such relationships are really in God, but they do not, in fact, have temporal implications. If this last alternative is the case, we are left with the original difficulty of explaining how a timeless creator can be related to temporal creatures. The first of these three options, based on the notion of a *relatio rationis tantum*, seems no more attractive than the latter two.

It may be objected that the above account of Thomas's notion of a *relatio rationis tantum* between God and creatures is based on an unjustified extension of Thomas's limited and technical sense of the term '*realis*'. That is, in contrasting *relatio rationis tantum* with *relatio realis*, Thomas does not mean to suggest that God is not, for example, "really" a creator, but only that God is not compelled to create; rather, he does so by a voluntary act of will.[29] Indeed, Thomas does explain the *relatio rationis tantum* as a relation in which one *relatum* is dependent on the other, but not

---

[28]"Operatio intellectus et voluntatis est in operante. Et ideo nomina quae significant relationes consequentes actionem intellectus vel voluntatis dicuntur de Deo ab aeterno. Quae vero consequuntur actiones procedentes secundum modum intelligendi ad exteriores effectus, dicuntur de Deo ex tempore, ut *Salvator*, *Creator*, et hujusmodi" 1a. 13, 7 ad 3 (B 3:76).

[29]"Non enim producit creaturas ex necessitate suae naturae, sed per intellectum et voluntatem, ut supra dictum est. Et ideo in Deo non est realis relatio ad creaturas. Sed in creaturis est realis relatio ad Deum, quia creaturae continentur sub ordine divino et in earum natura est quod dependeant a Deo" 1a. 28, 1 ad 3 (B 6:26).

vice versa.[30] If this narrower interpretation of *relatio rationis tantum* is correct, we may allow a more substantial relation between God and creatures than one that exists only in the human mind. We are, however, still left with the original difficulty of how such a relationship between timeless and temporal beings can be understood.

For these reasons, the notion of a *relatio rationis tantum*, although it may have other important functions, does not seem to help us understand how a timeless being can be related to temporal beings. Let us turn, therefore, to another of Thomas's tentative solutions to this problem.

ETERNITY AS
EVERLASTING DURATION

We noted in chapter one that several passages in the *Summa Contra Gentiles* appear to identify eternity with everlasting duration.[31] In another passage from the *Summa Theologiae*, Thomas claims that the divine eternity may be thought of as an everlasting imaginary time predating the world.[32] Such claims, if taken seriously, suggest that God's eternity may be better understood as everlasting temporal existence that as timelessness. This interpretation would seem to allow for the existence of divine volitional and creative acts in time, and thus enable a straightforward, temporal relation of God to creatures.

Like the use of the *relatio rationis tantum*, however, this approach to the problem of God's relation to creatures in will and action raises serious difficulties of its own. First of all, adoption of a view of eternity as everlasting existence would undermine the solution to the problem of reconciling divine omniscience and human freedom presented in chapter one. That solution required an

---

[30]"Quandocumque aliqua duo sic se habent ad invicem, quod unum dependet ab altero sed non e converso, in eo quod dependet ab altero, est realis relatio; sed in eo a quo dependet, non est relatio nisi rationis tantum" *de Ver.* 4, 5c (Marietti, 1953) 1:84.

[31]See chapter one above, n. 24, 9.

[32]See n. 12 above.

interpretation of eternity as timelessness in order to deny any temporal relation between God's knowledge and human action. Accepting everlasting temporal existence in God, then, would reintroduce all the problems of theological determinism.

In addition to jeopardizing human freedom, an everlasting or durational interpretation of eternity may also call the doctrine of *divine* freedom into question. This conclusion has recently been suggested by Richard La Croix in an essay entitled "Omniprescience and Divine Determinism."[33] La Croix argues that divine free will is incompatible with a cluster of other divine attributes including foreknowledge, omniscience, immutability, and eternity.

To ascribe foreknowledge, or knowledge of future events to God, La Croix points out, is to assume that future events can be known. Assuming omniscience as well implies that God must have knowledge of all future events; La Croix calls this property 'omniprescience'. The doctrine of divine immutability, La Croix argues, implies further that God never lacks the property of omniprescience. La Croix acknowledges the existence of two interpretations of eternity, namely, unending duration (or everlasting existence) and timelessness.[34] He adopts the former and applies it to the doctrine of divine omniprescience as follows: "God has knowledge of *all* future events at *every* moment of an indefinite stretch of time."[35] From this doctrine La Croix derives the following principle:

> (P1) For *any* act that God performs there is *no* time prior to that act at which God does *not* know that he will perform that act.[36]

At this point in his exposition, La Croix states and briefly defends several necessary conditions for the occurrence of a decision or free choice. First, he points out that decisions are typically in

---

[33] *Religious Studies* 12 (1976): 365-81.

[34] Ibid., 368-69.

[35] Ibid., 369.

[36] Ibid.

time and occur at particular times; therefore, there is a time prior to the decision at which no decision has yet been made. La Croix expresses this condition as follows:

(Q1)"x decides at T_2 to do a at T_3" entails "there is a time, T_1, prior to T_2, at which x has not yet decided with respect to doing a at T_3."[37]

Second, La Croix contends that an individual cannot both be un-decided with respect to performing some future act and at the same time know that he will perform that act. This condition is stated in general terms as follows:

(Q2)"x has not yet decided at T_1 with respect to doing a at T_3" entails "x does not know at T_1 whether or not he will do a at T_3."[38]

La Croix formulates the following argument based on (P1), (Q1), and (Q2):

(1) If it is possible for God to decide at T_2 to do a at T_3, then God has not decided at T_1 with respect to doing a at T_3 (by [Q1]). (2) If God has not yet decided at T_1 with respect to doing a at T_3, then God does not know at T_1 whether or not he will do a at T_3 (by [Q2]). (3) If it is possible for God to decide at T_2 to do a at T_3, then God does not know at T_1 whether or not he will do a at T_3 (from [1] and [2]). (4) It is false that God does not know at T_1 whether or not he will do a at T_3 (by [P1]). (5) It is not possible for God to decide at T_2 to do a at T_3 (from [3] and [4]).[39]

Since this argument applies to every moment of God's everlasting existence and to every act God performs, La Croix maintains that the cluster of doctrines he cites (foreknowledge, omniscience, im-mutability, unending duration) entail that it is impossible for God ever to make any decisions at all and that none of God's acts can be the result of his choosing to perform those acts.

How might this argument be challenged? (P1) clearly follows from La Croix's interpretations of the various divine attributes, and the argument itself seems valid. Two areas, however, are open to criticism. First, we may reject (Q1) and (Q2), La Croix's nec-

---

[37]Ibid., 371.

[38]Ibid., 372.

[39]Ibid., 373.

essary conditions for decision making, on the grounds that although these are necessary conditions of the finite, temporal decision making of creatures, there is no justification for ascribing them to God as well. This response, I think, is clearly able to block La Croix's argument. But adopting this line of criticism involves acknowledging that everlasting decision and action in God are just as difficult to explain as timeless decision and action. In other words, we must admit that interpreting the divine eternity as unending duration cannot help us give an account of divine will and action.

Second, we may accept (Q1) and (Q2), yet reject one or more of La Croix's interpretations of the divine attributes. But which ones? Thomas is clearly committed to the doctrines of omniscience and immutability.[40] If he accepts unending duration, he would seem to be committed to foreknowledge as well, and hence be unable to avoid La Croix's conclusion that God's will is not free. The interpretation of divine eternity as everlasting or unending duration does not, then, appear to give us a better account of the relation of divine will and action to creatures than the doctrine of timelessness.

WILL, ACTION, AND ANALOGY

We have already noted that for Thomas, will and action, like knowledge and the rest of the divine attributes, are predicated of God and human beings analogously. We cannot, therefore, simply draw inferences regarding the nature of divine will and action from our knowledge of human will and action. What knowledge we can have of these attributes depends on which elements of meaning are common and which differ in their different contexts. Some of the differences between the divine and human contexts are clearly recognizable. For example, the divine will is universal in scope while human wills are necessarily very limited. Also, the divine creative action needs no materials to produce its effects, while human products always require certain raw materials.

---

[40] 1a. 9, 1; 1a. 14, 11.

In this chapter we have concentrated on yet another difference between human and divine will and action. We have argued that the logic of the terms 'decision' and 'action' in human contexts entails that they occur in time. We have also argued that Thomas's doctrine cannot allow the ascription of temporality to divine will and action. Defenders of Thomas may point out that such differences must be expected, given the fact that these terms are predicated analogically of God and creatures. Acknowledging this basic difference, however, severely restricts the content of the common core of meaning, which makes these terms analogical rather than equivocal.

CHAPTER FOUR

HARTSHORNE'S DIPOLAR CONCEPTION OF GOD

I n this chapter I will consider a second conception of God that offers a means of reconciling the doctrines of divine omniscience and human freedom. This conception has been developed by Charles Hartshorne in a series of books and articles spanning more than forty-five years.[1] Though clearly indebted to Alfred North Whitehead's brief but highly suggestive remarks on the nature and role of God in his metaphysical system, Hartshorne's own conception of God differs from Whitehead's in several ways.[2] Unless otherwise noted, the discussion here will be restricted to Hartshorne's own more fully articulated doctrine of

[1]From *Beyond Humanism* (Chicago: Willett, Clark, and Co., 1937) to *Omnipotence and Other Theological Mistakes* (Albany: State University of New York Press, 1984).

[2]See *Two Process Philosophers: Hartshorne's Encounter with Whitehead*, ed. Lewis S. Ford (Tallahassee: American Academy of Religion, 1973).

God. As in the previous two chapters, I will first offer a brief statement of the doctrine and then examine several criticisms that have been directed against it.

OUTLINE OF THE DOCTRINE

As was noted in chapter one, Thomas reconciles divine omniscience and human freedom by contrasting the natures of God and the world in several fundamental ways. God is conceived as absolutely timeless, immutable, and independent of the world, while the world is wholly temporal, mutable, and dependent on God. Thomas distinguishes God and the world in a number of other ways as well: God is exclusively cause, creator, infinite, necessary, and simple; the world is exclusively effect, created, contingent, and composite. There are, of course, causes, necessary truths, and simple natures *within the world*, but all of these derive ultimately from God, who alone possesses ultimate and absolute causal power, necessity, and simplicity. Thomas's attribution of all these "absolute" predicates to God alone, Hartshorne claims, is based on a conception of perfection derived ultimately from the Greeks. On this view, the perfect being is complete, self-sufficient, immutable, and lacking no possible value.[3]

Hartshorne offers three reasons for rejecting this understanding of perfection. First, he argues that an absolute maximum of value cannot be actualized, since certain values are incompatible with one another.[4] Unlike the infinite array of possible values, then, any actual embodiment of value must be limited, or must limit itself.[5] Second, some values, such as beauty measured in terms of harmony, intensity, and richness, have no final or absolute maximum, according to Hartshorne.[6] Third, Hartshorne claims that certain attributes included in the classical conception

---

[3]Charles Hartshorne, *A Natural Theology for Our Time* (LaSalle IL: Open Court, 1967) 18-20.

[4]Hartshorne, *Creative Synthesis and Philosophic Method* (LaSalle IL: Open Court, 1970) 229.

[5]Ibid., 117.

[6]Ibid., 242-43.

of perfection, namely absolute immutability and independence, are in fact inappropriate to perfection, since they conflict with the ideals of love and care.[7] This claim is based on an account of love as including responsiveness to the changing needs of another.

In contrast to Thomas, then, Hartshorne rejects the ascription of the predicates 'timeless', 'immutable', 'independent', 'cause', 'creator', 'infinite', 'necessary', and 'simple' exclusively to God (in their absolute sense) and the contrary predicates exclusively to the world. Rather, Hartshorne bases his idea of God on the thesis that the relative or changeable must be attributed to God in addition to the absolute, immutable, and independent.[8] Hartshorne, then, seeks to ascribe the predicates in both of the above sets of contraries to God.

Since contrary predicates cannot consistently be ascribed to a single subject, Hartshorne distinguishes the abstract nature of God from his concrete states. In making this distinction, he denies Thomas's doctrine of the complete identification of essence and existence in God (and hence also Thomas's doctrine of the divine simplicity). For both Thomas and Hartshorne, attributes such as goodness, knowledge, and power belong necessarily to the divine nature. But in Hartshorne's view, these attributes are understood so as to allow their temporal expression in the successive concrete states of God. For example, though God always manifests supreme goodness, the particular way in which this goodness is manifested changes in response to changes in the world.

Thus the predicates 'eternal', 'independent', 'necessary', 'simple', and 'unchangeable' are ascribed to God's "primordial nature," the divine nature considered abstractly; their contraries are ascribed to God's "consequent nature," or God as a concrete existent.[9] God possesses his abstract nature eternally (everlast-

---

[7]Hartshorne, *The Divine Relativity* (New Haven: Yale University Press, 1948) 43.

[8]Ibid., ix.

[9]Though Hartshorne borrows the terms 'primordial nature' and 'consequent nature' from Whitehead, his interpretation of them differs significantly from Whitehead's.

ingly) and necessarily; it is independent of all influence, simple, and unchangeable. In contrast to this abstract nature, God's concrete existence, what Hartshorne calls the divine experience, is temporal, changing, and dependent on the world. Hence it also includes many contingent properties. By means of this distinction, Hartshorne can claim that God remains steadfast in all his essential attributes and still interacts with other beings, both influencing and being influenced by them.

Whatever its possible shortcomings, Thomas's account of God and the world does clearly establish God's transcendence of the world. But, Hartshorne asks, if God's transcendence is absolute and comprises the utter negation of all creaturely qualities, how can we conceive him at all or distinguish him from mere nothing?[10] Moreover, though attributes like immutability would clearly distinguish God from creatures, they do not clearly demonstrate his superiority or perfection.

Instead of the negation of all creaturely qualities, then, Hartshorne proposes a principle of the "dual transcendence" of the divine. According to this principle, transcendence is the possession of the highest achievable forms of both sets of metaphysical contraries. Consider, for example, the case of independence and dependence. While ordinary beings are dependent on only a limited number of others for their experience, the transcendent being depends on all other beings for the data of his experience. On the other hand, while ordinary beings cannot maintain their character or their existence under all circumstances, the transcendent being can adapt, without loss of any of his essential attributes, to any possible situation whatsoever. Thus each divine experience is universally open to influence, but the essential attributes of God persist through every change.[11] God therefore possesses both dependence and independence in eminent degree.

Hartshorne offers similar interpretations for the other predicates listed above, in each case attributing the highest form of both contraries to God. Of all individuals, his existence alone is

---

[10]Hartshorne, *Creative Synthesis and Philosophic Method*, 228.

[11]Ibid., 233.

necessary, an *a priori* implication of any existence whatsoever,[12] while God's actual states are supremely *contingent*, incorporating every contingent being. Likewise, God is the universal *creator* in his influence on the whole of existence and the universal *creature* in receiving the influences of all things.

In light of this "dipolar" conception of God, Hartshorne proposes an alternative to Thomas's account of perfection. Perfection is defined as "an excellence such that rivalry or superiority on the part of other individuals is impossible, but self-superiority is not impossible."[13] In this definition certain and universal superiority over others replaces the notion of an absolute maximum of value. Any stronger definition of perfection is, according to Hartshorne, neither possible for an individual being nor essential for religious faith. For instance, a major religious function of Thomas's doctrine of an absolute immutable perfection is to guarantee divine reliability in all circumstances, but this may be accomplished equally well by Hartshorne's notion of a perfectly adequate divine knowledge of and response to every worldly event.[14]

In view of his clear differences from Thomas, it is not surprising that Hartshorne also adopts a different approach to the problem of reconciling divine omniscience and human freedom. He argues that the free actions of creatures precede divine knowledge in time and are causally necessary for God's knowledge of them. The states of God's knowledge, therefore, must be temporally ordered and changing. Clearly, then, Hartshorne does not include all future contingent events in the divine knowledge. Like Clarke,[15] he contends that this does not jeopardize the perfection of divine knowledge, since the undetermined aspects of the future *cannot* be known until they occur. Moreover, Hartshorne uses an argument similar to Kretzmann's[16] to point out that a temporal

---

[12]Hartshorne, *The Divine Relativity*, 32.

[13]Ibid., 20.

[14]Ibid., 233.

[15]See chapter two, 42-45.

[16]Ibid., 37-42.

conception of divine knowledge permits one kind of "knowledge" that a timeless conception cannot.

Unlike the doctrine of timeless knowledge, in which God is said to know the whole temporal career of the world at once, Hartshorne's account allows God at each moment to know everything actual as actual, and everything possible as possible. The divine knowledge, therefore, is infinite in two ways: it includes an infinite number of past actualities, and it includes an infinite number of possibilities.

How does God become aware of every change that occurs in the world? Hartshorne claims that God is intimately related to each worldly event. He likens this relationship to the relationship of mind and body in human beings.[17] Through this analogy, Hartshorne seeks to emphasize the closeness of the God-world relationship and to indicate that the world is a part of God in much the same way as our bodies are a part of ourselves. The limits of this analogy, however, are also very important to note.

First, while human beings have no direct awareness of most of what is going on within their bodies, God is held to have a perfectly adequate awareness of each individual creature, akin to the relationship of an ideally vigilant and loving father to his children. Second, while most events occur outside ourselves (that is, outside our bodies), everything is within God: he has no external, but only an internal environment.[18] Third, while past events fade and are ultimately forgotten in human experience, nothing is lost from the divine consciousness. Rather, every past experience retains in God all the definiteness it possessed when it was present. The divine consciousness is, therefore, cumulative—though it continually gains new objects, it never loses the old ones. In it every event is preserved without loss.

Hartshorne interprets divine will, like divine knowledge, as an aspect of the temporal interaction of God and the world. He ex-

---

[17]Charles Hartshorne, "Analogy," in *An Encyclopedia of Religion*, ed. Vergilius Ferm (New York: Philosophical Library, 1945).

[18]Hartshorne therefore uses the term 'panentheism' ("all in God") to describe his theory. See *The Divine Relativity*, 88-92.

plicitly rejects Thomas's doctrine of a one-way causal relationship between God and the world with its implication that all power belongs ultimately to God. Hartshorne speaks instead of God's power as a kind of persuasion.

> All that God can directly give us is the beauty of his ideal for us, an ideal to which we cannot simply not respond, but to which our response has to be partly self-determined, and it has to be influenced by past creaturely responses in our universe. "Persuasion" is the ultimate power; not even God can simply coerce.[19]

This divine ideal for each creature is also the manifestation of God's love. As God's ideal influences creatures, so also do the creatures' decisions influence God: they do so by becoming the objects of the divine consciousness, where they are unified into a single vision. God must, therefore, experience some world, but what kind of world he experiences is determined by his own decisions along with those of creatures. Hartshorne also ascribes to divine will the determination of laws of nature for each cosmic epoch.[20] These laws form an apparently irresistible part of the divine ideal for each creature. They "set the stage" for creaturely activity, providing a basic harmony among creaturely actions and allowing those actions to be unified in the divine experience.

These are the main features of Hartshorne's conception of God. I turn now to a consideration of the critical response to that conception.

The atheist's strongest attack on theism, according to Hartshorne, is to argue that the very concept of God is incoherent, and hence it cannot be instantiated. Hartshorne's major goal, therefore, has been to develop a conception of God that is demonstrably coherent—free, that is, from logical inconsistency. Hartshorne also contends that this new conception of God has as much religious significance as its classical predecessors. Not surprisingly, critics have raised questions about both the coherence and the religious significance of Hartshorne's conception of God. We will consider several instances of both of these types of criticism.

---

[19]Hartshorne, *Creative Synthesis and Philosophic Method*, 239.

[20]Hartshorne, *A Natural Theology*, 53.

THE COHERENCE
OF THE DOCTRINE

In this section we will examine four major criticisms of the coherence of Hartshorne's doctrine of God. These four criticisms are as follows: (1) Hartshorne's conception of God is based on a faulty theory of knowledge, which requires that the knower include the known. (2) The tremendous number and variety of worldly existents cannot be unified in a single organic whole. (3) The infinite number of past and present events cannot be unified in a single state of knowledge. (4) Certain tenets of relativity physics are incompatible with Hartshorne's claim that God's experience unifies a simultaneous cross-section of the universe.

In separate analyses of Hartshorne's book, *The Divine Relativity*, Philip Phenix and John Wild both take issue with the theory of knowledge upon which Hartshorne's conception of God is based.[21] Hartshorne states this theory in no uncertain terms: "To include relations is to include their terms. Hence to know all is to include all."[22] This view makes knowledge a special case of Whitehead's general concept of prehension, the direct appropriation of a previous event, or as Hartshorne calls it, the "feeling of feeling," which is the ultimate form of all experience.[23] Both Phenix and Wild admit that knowledge involves a mental grasp of its object that does enrich and change the knower, but argue that knowledge does *not* require the literal or physical inclusion of the known within the knower.

Hartshorne replies to this criticism by stating that since all human knowledge is imperfect and incomplete, the known *is* external, but *only* to the extent that humans fail to know it adequately. Because divine knowledge is perfectly adequate, however, it can and does include its objects as parts of an all-inclusive

[21]Philip Phenix, "Review of *The Divine Relativity*," *Journal of Philosophy* 46 (1949): 591-97; John Wild, "The Divine Existence: An Answer to Mr. Hartshorne," *Review of Metaphysics* 4 (1950): 61-84.

[22]Hartshorne, *The Divine Relativity*, 76.

[23]Ibid., 28-29.

whole.[24] I believe that this reply can be convincing only if one accepts Hartshorne's assumption that knowledge is a special case of the general notion of prehension. In prehension, a (past) event is directly given to (present) experience.[25] Prehension, therefore, *always* implies the inclusion of some event. The difference, then, between the human and divine cases is just one of the extent and fashion in which events are included: *some* events are included *imperfectly* in human experience; *all* events are included *perfectly* in divine experience.

Whether Whitehead's notion of prehension does provide the best available foundation for a theory of knowledge cannot be answered here, for it is likely to involve a general evaluation of Whitehead's metaphysics, an enterprise that would require a book of its own. Phenix and Wild, at any rate, are clearly not disposed toward accepting prehension as the underlying mechanism of knowledge, nor are they likely to accept Hartshorne's defense of his doctrine of knowledge as inclusion. Supposing their claim that knowledge does not require inclusion of the known object is granted, how would this affect Hartshorne's theory? It would not by itself require abandonment of either the all-inclusive nature of God or of his perfect knowledge. What it would require is that these two doctrines not entail one another, but be thought of as separate attributes of God. Each of them, then, would stand or fall depending on its relation to other parts of Hartshorne's theory, in particular, perhaps, to his doctrine of divine perfection.

The second criticism is a more direct challenge to Hartshorne's doctrine of God as the all-inclusive reality. Phenix argues as follows:

> A study of the forms of organization actually observed in the world appears to reveal a definite limitation on the size and complexity which organisms may attain without becoming unstable. That the aggregate of all things (assuming that there is a meaning even to such a totality) should form a real organic unity is, from this point of view, next to impossible. It is one thing to assert, as experience indicates we should, that

[24]Hartshorne, "The Divine Relativity and Absoluteness: A Reply," *Review of Metaphysics* 4 (1950): 31-60.

[25]Hartshorne, *Creative Synthesis and Philosophic Method*, 91-92.

there are in nature tendencies or drives towards unification, or even existing systematic unities, quite another thing to insist, as Hartshorne does, that in some intelligible sense the aggregate of all things already *is* an organic whole.[26]

Henry Nelson Wieman puts the same criticism in more vivid terms.

> According to Hartshorne, the cosmos is God's body and this body has a "cosmic consciousness" that is the mind of God. . . . Since all the galactic systems, with their exploding stars and vast lifeless spaces in between, give no evidence of being organized like a biological organism fit to embody a conscious mind, this view is not accepted here.[27]

I am not aware of an explicit reply by Hartshorne to these attacks on the all-inclusive nature of God. Were he called on to defend that doctrine, I believe Hartshorne would first point out that the above arguments are probabilistic, based on a supposed dissimilarity between the structure of the universe as a whole and the structure of finite organic unities within our experience. In fact, the structure of the universe as a whole may not be so very different from the structure of organisms on earth, for there are (relatively) vast empty spaces within each of the atoms of a living body. Moreover, Hartshorne himself places strict limitations on his analogy between the cosmic unity and finite organic unities. For instance, one mark of divine transcendence for Hartshorne is precisely God's ability to unify in his experience events that cannot be unified by any creature. Hartshorne may also argue that his doctrine is no more difficult to imagine than Thomas's doctrine of divine ubiquity, given any reasonable interpretation of Thomas's claim that God exists in all things in substance, power, and presence.[28]

Finally, Hartshorne's argument for the existence of a transcendent cosmic consciousness is *a priori*, not inductive and prob-

---

[26]Phenix, "Review," 595.

[27]Henry Nelson Wieman, "Transcendence and 'Cosmic Consciousness'," in *Transcendence*, ed. H. W. Richardson and D. R. Cutler (Boston: Beacon Press, 1969) 157-58.

[28]1a. 8, 3.

abilistic. Relying on his own version of Anselm's ontological argument, Hartshorne claims that if the all-inclusiveness of God is conceivable, it must be a part of the divine nature.[29] Hartshorne appeals further to Whitehead's philosophy of organism for a demonstration of the conceivability of divine all-inclusiveness. If, therefore, Hartshorne's version of the ontological argument is valid *and* if his interpretation of Whitehead's metaphysics in its application to God is coherent (these are clearly no minor conditions), then the criticisms of Phenix and Wieman would be irrelevant to his position.

The third criticism is also directed against divine inclusiveness. Lewis Ford poses a problem for Hartshorne's doctrine that the divine *knowledge* is all-inclusive.[30] Ford points out that according to the process metaphysics accepted by Hartshorne, "Every actuality comes into being as the appropriation and integration of its causal antecedents. Every actuality requires causal antecedents, *ad infinitum*. Thus for present actualities to exist, there must be an infinite series of prior actualities."[31] Furthermore, since Hartshorne's God preserves each past actuality in all of its determinateness in the (finite) states of his consciousness,[32] "God must actively synthesize an infinity of individual differences."[33] But, Ford argues, it is impossible for any finite actuality (including any state of the divine consciousness) to perform such a synthesis.[34]

Since Hartshorne holds that space is finite but temporal process is infinite, this criticism would seem to present more serious

---

[29]Hartshorne, "Divine Absoluteness and Divine Relativity," in *Transcendence*, 165. Hartshorne's interpretation of the ontological argument is defended at length in his books *The Logic of Perfection* (LaSalle IL: Open Court, 1962) and *Anselm's Discovery* (LaSalle IL: Open Court, 1965).

[30]Lewis S. Ford, "In What Sense is God Infinite? A Process Perspective," *Thomist* 42 (1978): 1-13.

[31]Ibid., 5.

[32]Hartshorne, *The Divine Relativity*, 157-58.

[33]Ford, "In What Sense is God Infinite?," 6.

[34]Ibid.

problems for him than the previous one.[35] Though Hartshorne does admit that the problems involved here are "baffling," he offers the following explanation:

> The infinity of prior states is not a mere infinity of mutually independent items; for the just preceding state will have included all earlier ones in its own unity. So in a sense God is combining finites, not an infinite and a finite. The numerical infinity of the previous multiplicity is entirely embraced in the aesthetic unity of an experience.[36]

This explanation is not entirely satisfactory to Ford, however; he argues that the "aesthetic unity of an experience" to which Hartshorne appeals would seem to involve the transmutation or blurring of individual differences in order to highlight certain common features. Hartshorne could not admit such a loss of individual differences and still maintain his strongly held contention that God preserves the past in all of its determinateness. But it is not clear that God's act of unifying the past in his experience must involve loss of individual differences. Hartshorne would, I suspect, maintain that the divine experience is able to incorporate and to retain each new event without blurring or distortion. Thus every divine experience would inherit from the preceding divine experience a unification of all the past and add to this unification a perfect awareness of all just preceding events in the world. Since each individual experience involves only the addition of a finite number of events, the whole sequence seems no more unintelligible than the existence of a world with no beginning in time.

Hartshorne himself has long recognized a difficulty in defending the coherence of his conception of God against a fourth criticism.[37] Hartshorne claims that each divine experience includes a universe of simultaneous events, but as he and a number of others have pointed out, relativity physics contends that there is no unique meaning to the idea of a simultaneous cross-section of the

---

[35]Hartshorne, *Creative Synthesis and Philosophic Method*, 125.

[36]Ibid., 126.

[37]Hartshorne, "Whitehead's Idea of God," in *The Philosophy of Alfred North Whitehead*, ed. Paul A. Schilpp (Evanston and Chicago: Northwestern University Press, 1941) 545-46.

universe.[38] In other words, what events are simultaneous with a given event will differ for individuals in different inertial systems. If, however, God experiences one particular cross-section of events as simultaneous, it then becomes a datum for the next cross-section of events and thereby defines a privileged inertial system, contrary to relativistic principles.

In recent writings Hartshorne is still experimenting with possible remedies for this difficulty. In one place he suggests that a notion of "God here-now" replace "God now" as an expression of the divine experience.[39] Hartshorne withholds a full endorsement of this suggestion, however, for he recognizes that it would require the abandonment of a single linear succession of divine states, call into question the individuality of God, and probably require an extensive reinterpretation of his entire theory. Perhaps future work in physics or philosophy will suggest an answer to this serious difficulty; at present it remains unresolved.

THE RELIGIOUS VALUE OF THE DOCTRINE

While the critics in the previous section object to Hartshorne's conception of God on logical or scientific grounds, another and probably larger group of critics finds fault with that conception on theological or axiological grounds. This type of criticism usually contends that Hartshorne's God lacks certain attributes or values that are essential to a *religiously* adequate concept of God. Here we will consider particular criticisms based on the lack of an adequate understanding of five fundamental attributes in Hartshorne's conception of God: transcendence, omnipotence, freedom, goodness, and personhood.

---

[38]See, for example, John T. Wilcox, "A Question from Physics for Some Theists," *Journal of Religion* 40 (1961): 293-300; Lewis S. Ford, "Is Process Theism Compatible with Relativity Theory?" *Journal of Religion* 48 (1968): 124-35; Fredrick F. Fost, "Relativity Theory and Hartshorne's Dipolar Theism," in *Two Process Philosophers*, ed. Lewis Ford (Tallahassee: American Academy of Religion, 1973) 89-99.

[39]Hartshorne, *Creative Synthesis and Philosophic Method*, 123-24.

In *God in Exile*, a comprehensive and systematic study of atheism in modern thought, the respected Thomistic scholar Father Cornelio Fabro criticizes Whitehead and Hartshorne's doctrines of God.[40] In this lengthy book, Fabro undertakes the difficult task of tracing all the major forms of modern atheism back to a single origin in Descartes's approach to questions of human existence and knowledge in the *cogito*. Fabro views Descartes's approach as based on a "principle of immanentism," that is, a reliance on individual human consciousness as the foundation of being and knowledge.[41] This principle—which Fabro finds in positions as divergent as the empiricism of Hume, the idealism of Hegel, and the existentialism of Heidegger—is said to block the acceptance of any genuinely transcendent aspect of being, and in particular of an adequate concept of divine transcendence.[42]

Fabro views the doctrines of Whitehead and Hartshorne, then, as one step in a progression toward explicit atheism inspired by the principle of immanentism. More specifically, Fabro includes Whitehead and Hartshorne in a section entitled "The Religious Atheism of Anglo-American Empiricism."[43] Whitehead and Hartshorne are said to draw their inspiration from James's emphasis on experience, Bradley's idealism, and Alexander's theory of cosmic evolution. Their theoretical approach, Fabro contends, finds its culmination in the explicit atheism of Dewey.[44]

Part of Fabro's critique of Whitehead and Hartshorne seems to depend on their relation to the above philosophers and on the appropriateness of viewing this Anglo-American tradition as an inevitable progression toward atheism. This interpretation of the tradition, however, is largely arbitrary, dictated more by the systematic structure of Fabro's book (each part of which contains a

---

[40]Cornelio Fabro, *God in Exile: Modern Atheism*, trans. Arthur Gibson (Westminster MD: Newman Press, 1968).

[41]Ibid., 24.

[42]Ibid., 25.

[43]Ibid., 747.

[44]Ibid., 851-54.

progression from theism to atheism within a particular tradition) than by actual theoretical relationships among the philosophies discussed. It is not at all clear, for instance, why the principles adopted by these philosophers should culminate in Dewey's pragmatism rather than in the process metaphysics of Hartshorne.

Though his treatment of James, Bradley, Alexander, Whitehead, and Hartshorne is primarily descriptive, Fabro also offers critical comments on their different doctrines of God. Each of these philosophies is held to be an example of a "presumptive or inferential atheism," since the God affirmed in them is said to lack one or more attributes essential to an adequate concept of God.[45] Like the other doctrines treated in this section of the book, the major fault of Whitehead and Hartshorne is their lack of an adequate notion of divine transcendence. Fabro's requirement in this area is "that God be transcendent in himself and not merely the sum or totality of the world or immersed in it as a force, life, or universal Mind."[46] This requirement is violated by Whitehead and Hartshorne's claims that God and the world directly experience each other and that God includes the world within himself. Fabro describes their view as "the dispersion of God into the world," and he suggests that the notion of the creative evolution of the world threatens to usurp the place of God entirely.

> For certainly the emergent evolution of a world that "is making itself" God cannot constitute or substantiate any such possibility of an opening onto transcendence; it is sheer cosmic process and nothing more.[47]

Fabro is clearly correct in pointing out that the dipolar God does not satisfy his conception of transcendence. If it is shown that only this strong conception of transcendence can provide an adequate doctrine of God, then his charge that Whitehead and Hartshorne are "presumptive atheists" would be justified. Due perhaps to his reliance on this strong conception of transcendence, however, I believe that Fabro fails to appreciate fully the senses in

---

[45]Ibid., 45.

[46]Ibid., 44.

[47]Ibid., 833.

which Whitehead and Hartshorne's God does transcend the world. Fabro continually pushes Whitehead's views in the direction of Alexander's theory of God as an emergent ideal, the unactualized goal of the world.[48] He seems prone, therefore, to overlook claims made by Whitehead and more clearly by Hartshorne that God is himself an actual entity related to, but clearly distinct from, the world. Fabro draws attention to a passage in which Whitehead claims that "every actual entity, including God, is a creature transcended by the creativity which it qualifies,"[49] and argues that this conflicts with the claim that God is *causa sui*. But the statement that God is "transcended" contained in the above passage means only that past states of God are included in his present states. In this sense, then, God is transcended only by himself. It is true that God is not completely *causa sui* or independent of the world, as Fabro requires, but he is able to assimilate any and all worldly events in his own experience, and can therefore only be enriched, never endangered, by the ongoing process of the world. Furthermore, this divine activity is said to include knowledge, power, and love in eminent and unsurpassable degree.

Though Fabro finds the explicit assertion of a God-world interaction unacceptably limiting, Hartshorne has a twofold reply: (1) his theory can maintain a clear distinction between God and the world (that is, God is not in danger of "dispersion into the world"), and (2) any stronger conception of divine transcendence (in particular, Thomas's own concept of transcendence) is unable to provide an adequate account of the relationship of God and the world. Hartshorne could defend the first part of his reply by arguing that God can always be distinguished from the world by his unique and everlasting possession of the eminent forms of attributes like wisdom, power, and love. As to the second part of the reply, chapters two and three have suggested some of the problems

---

[48]In fact, at the end of his chapter on Whitehead, Fabro mistakenly ascribes to Whitehead a passage written by Samuel Alexander. See Ford, "In What Sense is God Infinite?," 1-2.

[49]Fabro, *God in Exile*, 823.

encountered by Thomas's own conception of God in accounting for the relationship between God and the world.

Where Fabro sees a threat to divine transcendence in Hartshorne's view of God's relation to the world, others point out a threat to divine power. E. L. Mascall observes that the dipolar God cannot satisfy a "minimal" definition of God as "the transcendent cause of extramental beings," since all beings are self-creating for Hartshorne.[50] Mascall is joined by Stephen Ely and Robert Neville in maintaining that God, like all other beings, is subject to the ultimate metaphysical principle of creativity.[51] That is, God is bound to experience all worldly events and to unify them into the greatest possible whole. Given these restrictions, God is clearly not omnipotent in an absolute sense. Rather, he shares power with all other beings. As a result, his creation is not *ex nihilo* nor could he have decided not to create.

Hartshorne admits that if omnipotence requires that God possess all the power there is, then his God is not omnipotent. But, he argues, if any creatures are free, then they must possess at least some power of their own; hence not all power is God's.[52] For those who grant the existence of creaturely freedom, then, Hartshorne proposes that omnipotence be defined as "the ideal case of power assuming a division of power."[53]

The defender of the classical doctrine may agree that God shares his power with other beings, but insist that all such sharing of the divine power must be the result of a choice freely made by God. Hartshorne, however, argues further that since creativity is a part of the divine nature, God cannot fail to create. Hence

[50]E. L. Mascall, *The Openness of Being* (London: Darton, Longman and Todd, 1971) 161.

[51]Ibid., 169; Stephen Ely, *The Religious Availability of Whitehead's God* (Madison: University of Wisconsin Press, 1942) 25; Robert Neville, "Experience and Philosophy: A Review of Hartshorne's *Creative Synthesis and Philosophic Method*," *Process Studies* 2 (1972): 61.

[52]Hartshorne, "Is Whitehead's God the God of Religion?" in *Whitehead's Philosophy* (Lincoln: University of Nebraska Press, 1972) 99.

[53]Ibid., 100.

Hartshorne does allow that God's power, like that of creatures, is defined by the ultimate metaphysical principle of creativity.

How might this view be defended against those who find it an unacceptable limitation? Consider the following two alternatives: (1) If, as Hartshorne contends, creativity is the fundamental *a priori* principle of reality, then the notion of a power that can contravene it must be unintelligible. (2) If, on the other hand, the principle of creativity is a basic principle of the world only and not of God, then the nature of divine power is completely and unalterably hidden from our understanding. Given a commitment to the principle of creativity, Hartshorne's conception of divine power seems clearly preferable to unintelligibility or ignorance. Likewise, if one acknowledges a different metaphysical principle as fundamental, one's conception of divine power would have to conform to that principle for the same reasons.

As the above discussion suggests, the idea of freedom is closely related to power. Let us turn now to an argument by John Wild that Hartshorne's account of the relationship of God and the world requires an unacceptably weak conception of divine freedom.[54] Wild emphasizes the importance of what he calls "spontaneity" for genuine freedom. He claims that the spontaneity or freedom of an action increases as the external constraints and the relation of the action to one's necessary ends decreases. Pure spontaneity, then, would require the perfect indifference of the actor to different alternatives for achieving the same end.

Wild sees this perfect freedom in the classical conception of God, whose decision to create makes no real difference to himself. In contrast, Wild points out that the spontaneous action of Hartshorne's God is limited in several ways, in particular by the autonomous decisions and actions of creatures and by an inner moral necessity, which obliges him to do what is best.[55] Neville also emphasizes these limitations in his description of Hartshorne's God as "bound by necessity in his essential nature, obliged to pay constant attention to all the rest of us, and limited

---

[54]Wild, "The Divine Existence," 72-78.

[55]Ibid., 77.

in his creativity to choosing between only those alternatives having equal maximal value."[56]

Wild and Neville are correct in pointing out that Hartshorne's God is limited in his actions by the free actions of others and by his necessary concern for their well-being and for his own. But Hartshorne claims that limitation of freedom in just these senses is necessary in order to include a genuine love for creatures in the divine nature. Genuine love for creatures would seem to require that God's action be guided by the actual situation of the creatures; complete indifference to that situation would seem to betray a lack of concern for creatures. Thus there must be limits on the divine freedom for Hartshorne. Though these limits are determined by the application of his metaphysical principles to God, they also provide a vital elucidation of the meaning of divine love. Hartshorne may, in turn, ask whether the Thomistic conception of divine freedom does not have similar problems. Given Thomas's claim that God possesses fundamental attributes like goodness and knowledge necessarily, it would seem that Thomas's God is not free to do evil or to forget about his creatures. Hartshorne also wonders how an immutable and independent God can be said to respond lovingly to the suffering and joy of his creatures.

Despite Hartshorne's emphasis on the divine love, several philosophers have raised questions regarding the *goodness* of the dipolar God. God's activity, according to Hartshorne, is a continual synthesis of worldly events into the greatest possible harmony. What reason is there to believe, asks Stephen Ely, that human values and aspirations are always fostered in this activity? "What is evil to us may appear, by virtue of contrast and synthesis, beautiful to God. Perhaps World Wars are the black spots necessary for the perfection of the divine painting."[57]

Ely also argues that the value God achieves in his all-inclusive experience is value only he can enjoy, since we as humans cannot escape our limited perspective.[58] Wieman presses this

---

[56]Neville, "Experience and Philosophy," 62.

[57]Ely, *Religious Availability of Whitehead's God*, 51.

[58]Ibid., 49.

criticism even further. All of the highest human values, he contends, are evil from the standpoint of "cosmic consciousness."

> . . . [Cosmic consciousness] recognizes no values other than satisfactions experienced in one's own body, because nothing exists outside of its own body. Love and justice are not values experienced in one's own body, like the taste of food and drink and other sensuous pleasures. Love and justice are experienced in the relations between persons. Since the "cosmic consciousness" has no interest in anything outside its own body, it can have no experience of love and justice.[59]

Further evidence for this claim, according to Wieman, is the fact that human life has existed on earth for only a very brief period of its history, and the fact that environments able to support a form of life like humanity are infinitesimal compared to the immense expanse of the universe.[60] Give the extreme rarity of its appearance, human life seems to be an aberration or evil rather than a value for God.

In response to Ely, Hartshorne argues that God possesses the perfect coincidence of altruism and self-interest. Since all creatures are parts of him and all have a place in his knowledge, he wills their happiness as elements in his own happiness. Success for God "could only be the maximizing of values in the beings known, since these values form the content of the divine value."[61] In order to prove egoism or cruelty in God, Hartshorne continues, "one must show that he has more to gain from creaturely suffering, as alternative to boredom, than the creatures and less to gain from creaturely happiness."[62] Hartshorne does, I think, have good reason for claiming that his God does not prefer creaturely suffering to creaturely happiness *in general*. But since God's concern is with the maximization of value, he may still will suffering in particular cases in order to promote a greater overall value. Some suffering of this nature, Hartshorne points out, may be attributed to

---

[59]Wieman, "Transcendence and 'Cosmic Consciousness'," 159.

[60]Ibid., 159-60.

[61]Hartshorne, "Is Whitehead's God the God of Religion?," 104.

[62]Ibid.

unavoidable conflicts of interest between creatures—these involve suffering and tragedy for both God and creatures.[63] In any case, God's concern to maximize creaturely value (and hence also his own value) may involve the suffering of particular individuals. The divine motivation, it seems, is broadly utilitarian.[64] It has, therefore, the same basic strengths and weaknesses in accounting for human values as classical utilitarianism has in ethical theory.

Hartshorne also suggests in his reply to Ely that persons should be willing to accept suffering for the good of others.[65] He argues that pure self-interest is not a rational end, since it is limited by human forgetfulness and ultimately by death. Instead, Hartshorne maintains, persons should identify themselves with God's everlasting preservation of the value of all creatures.[66] Hartshorne would, on this basis, grant Ely's claim that God's value cannot be shared fully by human beings. But the fact that God transcends the limits of any individual perspective does not weaken his goodness; rather, it is essential to an effective concern for creatures. Thus the divine life is shared by every creature (according to its ability) as that life "floods back into the world" to inspire new achievements.

Wieman's more radical charge that God can have no appreciation at all of interpersonal values seems to be based on too narrow an application of the mind-body analogy to God and the world. Wieman fails to consider the disanalogies between divine and human experience of the "body." Primary among these is the fact that God is aware of each individual within his body; owing to this, he can maintain an interest in each individual's desires, goals, and interaction with others rather than merely receive from that individual a more or less vague feeling whose source is unclear.

---

[63]Ibid., 106.

[64]This claim is defended at length in my paper "Mill and Hartshorne," *Process Studies* 9:3 (1981).

[65]Hartshorne, "Is Whitehead's God the God of Religion?," 105.

[66]Ibid.

That the world is included in God does not imply that all divine values resemble "the taste of food and drink and other sensuous pleasures." On the contrary, God is able to use his unsurpassable intellect to order worldly events in one harmonious whole. As nearly as it can be described, God's omniscient experience of the world would seem to combine the purest and most intense intellectual vision with the sensual immediacy of experiencing one's own body. On this view, values for God should most closely resemble those of self-conscious rational agents like human beings. Why then, Wieman may ask, do planets capable of sustaining human life make up such a tiny part of the universe? Given our pervasive ignorance in this area, it seems difficult to come to any conclusions. Even if human biological forms are quite rare, perhaps basic human values may be held by very different life forms. In any case, our present inability to see our basic values embodied in any very large part of the universe seems problematic for any attempt to ascribe goodness to a creator-God.

Finally, scholars have questioned Hartshorne's justification for ascribing personhood to his dipolar God. Both Mascall and Colin Gunton point out that Hartshorne describes God's activity in general categorical terms like 'becoming', 'prehending', and 'feeling'. These terms refer to automatic, involuntary processes that are common to all of reality, and hence it is difficult to think of them as activities characteristic of personhood. Gunton asks, "Merely because God is so constituted that everything that happens must make an impact on him—a kind of metaphysical sponge, infinitely absorbent—are we to say that he *loves* everything?"[67] This criticism relies on grounds similar to those of our earlier criticisms of divine freedom and goodness. In each of these criticisms, the underlying concern is that a God bound by Hartshorne's metaphysical principles is more like a blind and inexorable cosmic force than a free and loving being interacting with the world.

---

[67]Colin E. Gunton, *Becoming and Being* (Oxford: Oxford University Press, 1978) 220.

A response on behalf of Hartshorne should stress the fact that although the nature of God's interaction with the world is specified in certain ways (that is, God must experience the world, preserve its values, etc.), these are just the most eminent manifestations of the basic *a priori* forms of interaction, and they do not interfere with divine freedom. If human persons exemplify these metaphysical principles in limited ways, then the fact that God exemplifies the same principles most perfectly cannot count against the divine personhood. Rather, it would seem to be strong evidence *for* the claim that God is a person.

One strength of Hartshorne's theory is that it offers an explanation for God's interaction with the world. Freedom and love are attributed to God based on the nature of that interaction. Thus they need not depend on God's ability to choose whether or not to interact. Hartshorne claims that God's necessary virtues are only a formal framework for action, within which he makes innumerable free decisions based on his unsurpassable creative power.[68]

Hartshorne would likely allow that terms like 'power', 'freedom', 'goodness', and 'love' are used analogously in his account of God as well as in Thomas's. Nevertheless, Hartshorne contends that his metaphysical system is able to give a clearer and more adequate account of these divine attributes than any other. In fact, that system has, with one or two exceptions, provided persuasive responses to the criticisms discussed in this chapter.

---

[68]Hartshorne, "Divine Absoluteness and Divine Relativity," 167.

CHAPTER FIVE

SUMMARY
AND
CONCLUSIONS

C hapters one through four have addressed the problem of reconciling divine omniscience and human freedom and evaluated two promising solutions to that problem—the classical doctrine of St. Thomas Aquinas and the contemporary doctrine of Charles Hartshorne. In this final chapter I would like to summarize the arguments and conclusions already presented and offer some final reflections on the general problem and on the two solutions here proposed.

A REVIEW
OF THE ARGUMENTS

Chapter one considered two arguments designed to show that divine omniscience and human freedom are incompatible. The first argument is stated by Aquinas as an objection to his own claim that God knows contingent future events. According to this objection, if God knew that an event x will happen, x will happen, since the possession of knowledge implies the truth of what is known. But "God knew that x will happen" is necessarily true, since God's knowledge is perfect and located in the past. Therefore, "x will happen" is necessarily true; that is, all events, including all human actions, occur necessarily and not contingently.

In reply to this objection, Thomas argues that the statement "God knew that x will happen" is false, since all events are eternally *present* to the divine gaze. With this response Thomas appears to reject the view that God has *foreknowledge* of worldly events. Thomas defines eternity as the mode of existence of the immutable, but he offers no clear answer to the question whether the divine eternity should be viewed as timeless existence (existence "outside of time") or everlasting existence (existence at all times). The interpretation of eternity as everlasting existence permits a sense of foreknowledge, since it implies that God's knowledge of an event exists at a time prior to the event's occurrence in the world. In order, therefore, to avoid the conclusion that all events are rendered necessary by divine foreknowledge, Thomas must commit himself to the view that God's knowledge is timeless, lacking any temporal relation to the events known.

The second argument for the incompatibility of divine omniscience and human freedom considered in chapter one is stated by Nelson Pike. Pike's argument differs from Thomas's in focusing directly on the freedom of human actions. It assumes that an action is free if it is within one's power to refrain from performing that action. Pike concludes that it is not within one's power to refrain from actions foreknown by God. This conclusion is based on the claim that it is not within one's power to bring about a change in past states of the divine knowledge. Pike contends that the conclusion of his argument may be avoided by claiming that God's knowledge is timeless.

Based on an analysis of these two arguments, I have maintained that only the doctrine of timelessness can make Thomas's view of an immutable divine knowledge of all things compatible with human freedom (in the libertarian sense). If, however, the assumption that God's knowledge is immutable is abandoned, another alternative is possible. This alternative, proposed by Charles Hartshorne, places God's knowledge in time and maintains that God knows human free actions only as they occur. On this view, God's knowledge is his all-inclusive and ever-growing experience of the world.

The next three chapters are devoted to an evaluation of Thomas's and Hartshorne's solutions to the problem of reconciling divine omniscience and (a libertarian conception of) human freedom. Chapter two considers the doctrine of a timeless divine knowledge, chapter three the doctrine of a timeless divine will and action, and chapter four the doctrine of divine knowledge as all-inclusive experience in time. Each of these chapters contains an outline of the doctrine and an analysis of recent critical reaction to that doctrine.

One of the strongest criticisms of divine knowledge considered in chapter two takes issue with the claim that timeless knowledge is a state of perfection. W. Norris Clarke proposes that change be ascribed to the divine consciousness in order to account for a genuine personal relationship between God and man. He argues that this in no way compromises the divine perfection; but, in fact, this suggestion is not compatible with Thomas's notion of perfection, since for Thomas perfection implies complete actuality and immutability.

Hartshorne also considers immutable knowledge a less than perfect state. He takes issue, in particular, with Thomas's analogy of the relation between God and creatures in which God is likened to an inanimate object of knowledge rather than an active human knower. Implicit in both Hartshorne and Clarke's criticisms is a rejection of Thomas's doctrine of perfection as a state of pure actuality and immutability.

At the end of chapter two, I examined Thomas's doctrine of analogy as a defense against the above criticisms. According to that doctrine, terms predicated of both God and man share certain elements of meaning, but differ in others. This doctrine, therefore, may be invoked to claim that in some cases the meaning of a term drawn from human experience is not fully applicable to God. Yet the success of this defense is achieved at the cost of making the divine nature more and more inaccessible to human understanding.

In chapter three it is argued that Thomas encounters difficulty in explaining the relation between the timelessness of di-

vine will and creation and their temporal effects. Recent analyses
of action interpret the relationship between will and action and
between actions and their results in causal terms. Our understanding of causal relationships, however, is based on the assumption that causes are always locatable in time either prior to
or simultaneous with their effects. Human conceptions of action
and causation, therefore, do not seem able to account for a timeless action with temporal results. Thomas appears to be bothered
by this limitation, for he suggests two other explanations for divine will and action. In view of the difficulties surrounding both
of those explanations, however, it appears that Thomas must conclude that divine will and action differ fundamentally from human will and action. Once again, the doctrine of analogy may be
invoked to explain this difference, with the result that human understanding of divine will and action is severely limited.

In chapter four I reviewed a number of challenges to both the
coherence and the religious significance of Hartshorne's dipolar
conception of God. Probably the most serious problem regarding
the coherence of Hartshorne's doctrine is the fact that it appears
to require that an absolute simultaneity of events be present in
the divine experience. This result conflicts with a vital tenet of
relativity theory: there is no unique simultaneity between individuals in different inertial systems.

The strongest criticisms of the religious adequacy of Hartshorne's doctrine of God contain a single underlying theme. They
argue that because God is subject to general metaphysical principles, this places unacceptable limitations on his transcendence,
power, and freedom. These criticisms are correct in pointing out
that Hartshorne puts limitations on the notions of divine transcendence, power, and freedom that are not present in Thomas's
doctrine of God. Hartshorne replies that his account does not seriously compromise any of the divine attributes and that some
limitations must be placed on the meaning of individual attributes in order to provide a coherent and complete doctrine of God.

THE STATE OF THE
CONTROVERSY

What general conclusions may be drawn from this study of the
problem of reconciling divine omniscience and human freedom? I

believe that the following two initial conclusions are clearly in order: (1) The problem itself is genuine and serious for anyone who
holds a libertarian view of human freedom. (2) The two approaches adopted by Thomas and Hartshorne are each able to resolve the problem successfully, though in very different ways.

I have tried to show that both theories possess considerable re-
sources for answering their critics. This is not surprising, given
the scholarly support for each theory, but it does make a reasoned
choice between them more difficult. The tremendous reach of the
theories defended by Aquinas and Hartshorne contributes to the
difficulty of choosing between them. Since each is nothing less
than a fully developed theologico-metaphysical system with God
as its key concept, doubts about a particular feature of the system
may not seem weighty enough to justify rejection of the entire system. What is needed, then, are criteria general enough to undertake the evaluation of such all-inclusive systems.

While many philosophers, especially in the twentieth century,
have doubted the existence of such criteria (logical positivists and
some linguistic analysts, for example), there is now a growing con-
viction that metaphysical systems can be evaluated, and a number of criteria have been proposed. In the rest of this chapter I will
focus on three such criteria that are presupposed by many of the
criticisms we have considered—namely, internal consistency, conceivability, and harmony with other areas of knowledge and experience, including science and religion.[1] I will use my own
interpretation and weighting of these criteria to defend my choice
between these two theories, recognizing that both theories (and
all of their rivals) have apparent weaknesses, and that different
criteria, or different interpretations of the same criteria, might
lead to a different result.

The major problem addressed in this study, reconciling divine
omniscience and human freedom, is a problem of *consistency*, or of
showing how these two doctrines can coexist without contradict-
ing one another. Here, as elsewhere, we seek consistency on the
grounds that a system generating internally inconsistent or im-

---

[1]Ferré offers similar criteria, including consistency, coherence, and appli-
cability to experience. See *Language, Logic and God* (New York: Harper and Row,
1961) 162-63.

possible results must be flawed. Both theories were able to avoid a potential inconsistency on this count, Thomas by insisting on divine timelessness and Hartshorne by denying divine foreknowledge of free actions. Thomas's theory was also defended against claims of inconsistency among the divine attributes made by Coburn, Kretzmann, and La Croix. Hartshorne's theory was defended against Ford's assertion of the impossibility of divine knowledge of an infinite past. In sum, both theories take great pains to demonstrate their internal consistency. I have tried to show ways in which both can be successfully defended against challenges to their consistency.

Consistency, however, is only one essential criterion of metaphysical systems; the different manner in which Aquinas and Hartshorne defend the consistency of their systems has different results for a second criterion, *conceivability*. If our goal is understanding of the basic structure of reality, then we must at least be able to formulate some idea of the principles and entities postulated by a theory. A theologian may at this point object that the goal of a theological system is not better understanding but stronger faith. Faith, however, requires some measure of understanding if it is to be meaningful and reasoned rather than empty and blind. Thus theology too depends on the conceivability of its theories.

Thomas defends his theory of God by postulating fundamental differences between divine and human attributes. God is, in other words, a supreme exception to all the categories of created existence. This investigation has focused largely on one example of these differences between God and the world, namely, the divine timelessness. Though timeless knowledge and timeless will are not inconsistent doctrines, we can conceive them only in the barest formal manner. We were even less successful in formulating a conception of the causal relationship between God's timeless will and action and its temporal results. Despite his efforts in the *Summa Theologiae* to provide a doctrine of the divine nature based on natural reason, then, Thomas is unable to say very much about God except what he is *not*. The less we can understand about God, however, the less confident we can be in acknowledging his existence as the supreme being.

Hartshorne, in contrast, seeks to explain the divine nature as the supreme embodiment of his universal metaphysical principles. God is not an exception to the categories of created existence; rather, he shares the basic modes of knowledge, experience, and action. Hartshorne's system has the advantage of providing a clearer, fuller conception of the divine nature. Nevertheless, some features, such as God's constant interaction with all other existents and his perfect retention of all past events in memory, still remain largely beyond human conception.

The final criterion, *harmony with other areas of knowledge and experience*, is based on the belief that a theory of unlimited generality should not conflict with other fundamental areas of human endeavor. I will focus on two areas from which criticisms have been directed against the two theories, namely, science and religion.

In radically separating the divine realm from the physical world of space and time, Thomas renders his theory invulnerable to scientific criticism, since science is confined to the physical world. Hartshorne, however, by using concepts of space and time to explain divine interaction with world, invites a comparison of his understanding of these concepts with that of the sciences. We have, in fact, defended Hartshorne against claims by Phenix and Wieman that the structure of the world does not support the existence of an all-inclusive deity. A more troubling problem, as Hartshorne acknowledges in his foreword to this volume, is the apparent inconsistency between the denial of simultaneity in relativity physics and Hartshorne's assertion that God experiences a simultaneous cross-section of the universe. As Hartshorne also points out, however, contemporary physics has not definitively resolved this issue; he has argued elsewhere that an accepted principle of quantum physics, Bell's theorem, provides support for the process conception of time.[2] The consistency of Hartshorne's view with scientific theory may thus depend on the outcome of this controversy within science.

---

[2]Charles Hartshorne, "Bell's Theorem and Stapp's Revised View of Space-Time," *Process Studies* 7 (1977): 183-91.

Finally, we have considered criticisms of both theories on the grounds of religious adequacy. A theory of ultimate reality will be acceptable to a religious tradition or community of faith only if it does not contradict, but rather supports and elucidates the religious experience and the fundamental tenets of that faith. Since both Aquinas and Hartshorne offer theistic systems, we may ask whether their systems are harmonious with major theistic religions such as Judaism, Christianity, and Islam.

A major criticism brought against the Thomistic system by Clarke and Hartshorne held that the concept of an immutable God unrelated to his creatures cannot do justice to the religious experience of God as a loving person who seeks a personal relationship with his creatures. God, according to this argument, cannot be completely separated from time and unconcerned with the temporal world, since the central theme of faith is God's saving action *in* history, recorded in the Scriptures and perhaps most vividly exemplified by the Christian belief in God's physical presence on earth in the person of Jesus Christ. The Incarnation, of course, is a mystery of faith that is not explained by Aquinas or Hartshorne (or any other theoretical system). Aquinas's view of God as timeless, immutable, and independent of the world, however, would seem to place a tremendous gulf between the divine nature and the Christ of faith. I also concluded that Thomas's doctrine of the divine will as ordering all things would, even if it is conceived as a timeless will, conflict with the doctrine of human freedom and hence with a response to the problem of evil based on man's free choice of evil.

A number of writers cited here also question the religious significance of Hartshorne's concept of God. These criticisms share a general concern that Hartshorne's account of the divine nature in terms of his general metaphysical principles places unacceptable limitations on the divine attributes of transcendence, omnipotence, freedom, goodness, and personhood. Hartshorne responds by noting that possession of attributes like transcendence and omnipotence in absolute degree would place limitations of a different sort on God; that is, it would interfere with God's ability to interact with the world or to share power with the creatures. Thus a God who is absolutely transcendent and omnipotent is less worthy of worship and love than one who is present to his creatures in a guiding but noncoercive way. God's goodness and love are thus expressed, for Hartshorne, in his interactions with the world. God could not choose not to support the world, but is this an unacceptable limitation on his freedom? A stronger sense of freedom would seem to conflict with God's steadfast love and concern for his creatures. For this reason, Hartshorne rejects Thomas's ascription of attributes like transcendence, omnipotence, omniscience, and immutability to God in absolute degree on the grounds that this view is not necessary for religious faith or worship; in fact, it interferes with the religiously fundamental doctrines of divine goodness and personal love.

The foregoing analysis should make clear my preference between the two theories. Despite the fact that both theories are internally consistent, Hartshorne's account of the divine nature is more attractive on the grounds of its greater conceivability and religious adequacy. My conclusion, of course, depends on several presuppositions, including the legitimacy of these criteria for a general evaluation of the two theories. For Thomas, applying the newly discovered and powerful Aristotelian theories to a milieu in which Christian faith was largely taken for granted, emphasis on the divine transcendence may have been the most fitting way to glorify God. For better or worse, however, the almost universal faith of the Middle Ages has disappeared, and the rationality of traditional religious belief has come under ever-increasing attack. Against this climate of skepticism, Hartshorne's emphasis on an explicit articulation of the concept of God and a defense of its conceivability is, I believe, a more appropriate response than Thomas's emphasis on how far the divine nature is beyond human comprehension.

BIBLIOGRAPHY

PRIMARY SOURCES

I. St. Thomas Aquinas

Commentum in Primum Librum Sententiarum Magistri Petri Lombardi (1 *Sent.*). Volume Six of *Opera Omnia*. Parmae, 1856.

De Veritate (*de Verit.*). In *Quaestiones Disputatae*. Volume One. Taurini: Marietti, 1953. English translation by Robert W. Mulligan, S. J. Chicago: Regnery, 1952.

Summa Contra Gentiles (*Cont. Gent.*). Taurini: Marietti, 1934.

Summa Theologiae. Sixty volumes. Blackfriars edition. New York: McGraw-Hill, 1964-1976.

II. Other Classical Sources

Alexander of Hales. *Summa Theologica*. Volume One. Quaracchi, 1924.

Aristotle. *De Interpretatione*.

——————————. *Physica*.

Augustine of Hippo. *De Civitate Dei*. English translation by Marcus Dods. New York: Modern Library, 1950.

——————————. *De Libero Arbitrio*. English translation by Anna S. Benjamin and L. H. Hackstaff. Indianapolis: Bobbs-Merrill, 1964.

———— ——————. *De Praedestinatione Sanctorum*. English translation by Peter Holmes and Robert E. Wallis. In *Saint Augustine: Anti-Pelagian Writ-*

ings. Volume Five of Library of the Nicene and Post-Nicene Fathers. Edited by Philip Schaff. New York: Christian Literature Co., 1887.

Boethius. *De Consolatione Philosophiae.*

Bonaventure. *Commentarius in Primum Librum Sententiarum Magistri Petri Lombardi.* Volume One of *Opera Omnia.* Quaracchi, 1882.

III. Charles Hartshorne

"Analogy." In *An Encyclopedia of Religion.* Edited by Vergilius Ferm. New York: Philosophical Library, 1945.

Anselm's Discovery. LaSalle IL: Open Court, 1965.

"Bell's Theorem and Stapp's Revised View of Space Time." *Process Studies* 7 (1977): 183-91.

Beyond Humanism. Chicago: Willett, Clark and Co., 1937.

Creative Synthesis and Philosophic Method. LaSalle IL: Open Court, 1970.

"Divine Absoluteness and Divine Relativity." In *Transcendence.* Edited by H. W. Richardson and D. R. Cutler. Boston: Beacon Press, 1969.

The Divine Relativity. New Haven: Yale University Press, 1948.

"The Divine Relativity and Absoluteness: A Reply." *Review of Metaphysics* 4 (1950): 31-60.

Insights and Oversights of Great Thinkers: An Evaluation of Western Philosophy. Albany: State University of New York Press, 1982.

"Is Whitehead's God the God of Religion?" In *Whitehead's Philosophy.* Lincoln: University of Nebraska Press, 1972, 99-110.

The Logic of Perfection. LaSalle IL: Open Court, 1962.

A Natural Theology for Our Time. LaSalle IL: Open Court, 1967.

Philosophers Speak of God. Edited by Charles Hartshorne and William Reese. Chicago: University of Chicago Press, 1953.

Reality as Social Process. Glencoe IL: Free Press, 1953.

"Whitehead's Idea of God." In *The Philosophy of Alfred North Whitehead.* Edited by Paul A. Schilpp. Evanston and Chicago: Northwestern University Press, 1941, 513-59.

SECONDARY SOURCES

Cahn, Steven M. *Fate, Logic, and Time.* New Haven: Yale University Press, 1967.

Castañeda, Hector-Neri. "Omniscience and Indexical Reference." *Journal of Philosophy* 64 (1967): 205-10.

Chapman, Tobias. "Determinism and Omniscience." *Dialogue* 9 (1970): 366-73.

Clarke, W. Norris, S. J. "A New Look at the Immutability of God." In *God Knowable and Unknowable*. Edited by Robert J. Roth. New York: Fordham University Press, 1973, 43-72.

Cobb, John B. *A Christian Natural Theology Based on the Thought of Alfred North Whitehead*. Philadelphia: Westminster Press, 1965.

Coburn, Robert C. "Professor Malcolm on God." *Australasian Journal of Philosophy* 41 (1963): 143-62.

Danto, Arthur. *Analytical Philosophy of Action*. Cambridge, Cambridge University Press, 1973.

Donceel, Joseph, S. J. "Second Thoughts on the Nature of God." *Thought* 46 (1971): 346-70.

Ely, Stephen. *The Religious Availability of Whitehead's God*. Madison: University of Wisconsin Press, 1942.

Fabro, Cornelio. *God in Exile: Modern Atheism*. Translated by Arthur Gibson. Westminster MD: Newman Press, 1968.

Ferré, Frederick. *Language, Logic and God*. New York: Harper and Row, 1961.

Ford, Lewis S. "In What Sense is God Infinite? A Process Perspective." *Thomist* 42 (1978): 1-13.

_____. "Is Process Theism Compatible with Relativity Theory?" *Journal of Religion* 48 (1968): 124-35.

_____, editor. *Two Process Philosophers: Hartshorne's Encounter with Whitehead*. Tallahassee: American Academy of Religion, 1973.

Fost, Fredrick F. "Relativity Theory and Hartshorne's Dipolar Theism." In *Two Process Philosophers: Hartshorne's Encounter with Whitehead*. Edited by Lewis S. Ford. Tallahassee: American Academy of Religion, 1973, 89-99.

Goldman, Alvin I. *A Theory of Human Action*. Englewood Cliffs NJ: Prentice-Hall, 1970.

Grünbaum, Adolf. "Time, Irreversible Processes, and the Status of Becoming." In *Problems of Space and Time*. Edited by J. J. C. Smart. New York: Macmillan, 1964, 397-425.

Gunton, Colin E. *Becoming and Being*. Oxford: Oxford University Press, 1978.

Helm, Paul. "Divine Foreknowledge and Facts." *Canadian Journal of Philosophy* 4 (1974): 305-15.

_____. "Timelessness and Foreknowledge." *Mind* 84 (1975): 516-27.

Hick, John. *Evil and the God of Love*. Second edition. London: Macmillan, 1977.

Hughes, G. E. and M. J. Cresswell. *An Introduction to Modal Logic*. London: Methuen, 1968.

Journet, Charles. *The Meaning of Evil*. Translated by Michael Barry. London: Geoffrey Chapman, 1963.

Kane, Robert H. "Divine Foreknowledge and Causal Determinism." *Southwestern Journal of Philosophy* 9 (1978): 69-76.

Kelly, Anthony J. "God: How Near a Relation?" *Thomist* 34 (1970): 191-229.

Kenny, Anthony. "Divine Foreknowledge and Human Freedom." In *Aquinas*. Edited by Anthony Kenny. London: Macmillan, 1969, 255-70.

Klubertanz, George P., S. J. *St. Thomas Aquinas on Analogy*. Chicago: Loyola University Press, 1960.

Kretzmann, Norman. "Omniscience and Immutability." *Journal of Philosophy* 63 (1966): 409-21.

La Croix, Richard. "Omniprescience and Divine Determinism." *Religious Studies* 12 (1976): 365-81.

McCann, Hugh. "Volition and Basic Action." *Philosophical Review* 83 (1974): 451-73.

Madden, Edward H. and Peter H. Hare. *Evil and the Concept of God*. Springfield IL: Charles C. Thomas, 1968.

Martin, R. M. "On God and Primordiality." *Review of Metaphysics* 29 (1976): 497-522.

Mascall, E. L. *The Openness of Being*. London: Darton, Longman, and Todd, 1971.

Minkowski, H. "Space and Time." In *Problems of Space and Time*. Edited by J. J. C. Smart. New York: Macmillan, 1964, 297-312.

Moskop, John C. "Mill and Hartshorne." *Process Studies* 9:3 (1981): 18-33.

Neville, Robert. "Experience and Philosophy: A Review of Hartshorne's *Creative Synthesis and Philosophic Method*." *Process Studies* 2 (1972): 49-67.

O'Connor, D. J. *Free Will*. Garden City NJ: Doubleday, 1971.

Ogden, Schubert M. *The Reality of God*. New York: Harper and Row, 1966.

Phenix, Philip. Review of *The Divine Relativity* in *Journal of Philosophy* 46 (1949): 591-97.

Pike, Nelson. "Divine Foreknowledge, Human Freedom, and Possible Worlds." *Philosophical Review* 86 (1977): 209-16.

——————. "Divine Omniscience and Voluntary Action." *Philosophical Review* 74 (1965): 27-46.

——————. *God and Timelessness*. New York: Schocken Books, 1970.

Pittenger, W. Norman. *God in Process*. London: SCM Press, 1967.

Plantinga, Alvin. *God, Freedom, and Evil*. New York: Harper and Row, 1974.

_____. *The Nature of Necessity*. Oxford: Clarendon Press, 1974.

Prior, A. N. "The Formalities of Omniscience." *Philosophy* 37 (1962): 114-29.

Saunders, John Turk. "Of God and Freedom." *Philosophical Review* 75 (1966): 219-25.

Schlick, Moritz. "The Four Dimensional World." In *Problems of Space and Time*. Edited by J. J. C. Smart. New York: Macmillan, 1964, 292-96.

Smart, J. J. C., editor. *Problems of Space and Time*. New York: Macmillan, 1964.

Stokes, Walter E., S. J. "Whitehead's Challenge to Theistic Realism." *New Scholasticism* 38 (1964): 1-21.

Taylor, Richard. "Prevention, Postvention, and the Will." In *Freedom and Determinism*. Edited by Keith Lehrer. New York: Random House, 1966, 65-85.

Whitney, Barry L. "Divine Immutability in Process Philosophy and Contemporary Thomism." *Horizons* 7 (1980): 49-68.

Wieman, Henry Nelson. "Transcendence and 'Cosmic Consciousness'." In *Transcendence*. Edited by H. W. Richardson and D. R. Cutler. Boston: Beacon Press, 1969.

Wilcox, John T. "A Question from Physics for Some Theists." *Journal of Religion* 40 (1961): 293-300.

Wild, John. "The Divine Existence: An Answer to Mr. Hartshorne." *Review of Metaphysics* 4 (1950): 61-84.

Williams, Donald C. "The Myth of Passage." *Journal of Philosophy* 48 (1951): 457-72.

Wittgenstein, Ludwig. *Philosophical Investigations*. Oxford: Blackwell, 1953.

MUP *Divine Omniscience and Human Freedom*

Binding designed by Alesa Jones

Interior typography design by Margaret Jordan Brown

Composition by MUP Composition Department

Production specifications:
    text paper—60 pound Warren's Olde Style
    endpapers—Legendry Pearl
    cover—(on .088 boards) Joanna Arrestox B 312000
    dust jacket—Printed one color PMS 455 (charcoal gray) on Legendry
    Pearl

Printing (offset lithography) by Omnipress of Macon, Inc., Macon,
    Georgia

Binding by John H. Dekker and Sons, Inc., Grand Rapids, Michigan